Praise for *Finding My Course*

In Finding My Course, Tracy Hanson offers a raw, deeply moving exploration of resilience, healing, and the long journey toward wholeness. In beautifully told short stories and with unflinching honesty, she invites us into the moments that shaped her—both the triumphs and the wounds—while weaving a narrative of perseverance, grace, and transformation. This is more than a memoir; it's a testament to the power of naming our truth, reckoning with our past, and stepping into a future marked by courage and hope. Hanson's story is a gift to anyone longing to find meaning in their own journey.

— **Chuck DeGroat,** professor and executive director in the Clinical Mental Health Counseling Program at Western Theological Seminary, Holland, Michigan; author of *Healing What's Within: Coming Home to Yourself and to God When You're Wounded, Weary, and Wandering.*

Team captain. Golf prodigy. Valedictorian. So many highs matched by crushing lows and a vulnerability rarely seen. This small-town girl from Northern Idaho shares her All-American, divot-eating, Curtis Cup, LPGA-playing life story—a life of redemption. *Finding My Course* will tear at your heart.

— **Jim Murphy,** performance coach, retreat leader, author of *Inner Excellence: Train Your Mind for Extraordinary Performance and the Best Possible Life*

Tracy Hanson opens her heart and bravely shares her story to help others in the journey from trauma to healing. She shows us that while we can't change the past, we can come to terms with the valleys. And in doing so, we can find hope and learn to love ourselves just as God loves us. It is only through deep exploration and understanding that healing can truly begin. *Finding My Course* is a story of courage, perseverance, and hope through God's love. Tracy's journey to health and healing is inspiring and offers light to those who are hurting.

— **Leta Lindley,** LPGA and Legends of the LPGA Tour professional; champion of the 2024 U.S. Women's Senior Open

Tracy Hanson's life story is a remarkable testament to resilience and true grit, intricately woven with the grace, mercy, and providence of God. Many aspects of her journey are deeply relatable, serving as a powerful reminder that the Lord is always by our side, never leaving or forsaking us, but leading us to healing and wholeness through Him.
— **Meredith Kirk**, LPGA Teaching professional and LINKS Players Women's National Director

Tracy Hanson's story captivated me more with every page. I loved learning about her journey in sports, from basketball to golf, and even her brief experience with volleyball. But what truly stands out is Tracy's courage in sharing painful experiences and how she learned the truth about them, and herself. In *Finding My Course* the way she faces the issues while beautifully growing in Christ is truly eye-opening and will resonate deeply with anyone with similar experiences. Tracy's story is both inspiring and impactful and I hope that it encourages others to speak up.
— **Geremy Davis**, former NFL player, founder/CEO of Golf and Gospel LLC

Finding My Course is a story of perseverance, hope and God's grace. Hebrews 13:5 states that "God has said, 'Never will I leave you; never will I forsake you.'" This is evident throughout Tracy's journey. Instead of taking the circumstances that could so easily have broken her down and hardened her heart forever, Tracy lets God use her life for a purpose: Overcoming the stigmas surrounding trauma to help guide, counsel, and love those around her.
— **Carly Umlauf**, Generation Z lover of books, wife, and career woman

Finding My Course is the compelling story of a gritty, competitive, fiercely brave little girl who became a world-class athlete and a courageous steward of truth, hope and her talents. With a style that's refreshingly authentic,

witty, and relatable, Tracy Hanson shares a poignant journey through the excruciatingly complicated dynamics of exploitation and trauma, in which she channeled her extraordinary tenacity into slowing down and pursuing health and healing.
— **Mindy Pierce**, L.P.C., GROW Counseling, Atlanta, Georgia

Tracy Hanson's story is a powerful reminder of the transformative journey toward discovering our true identity and self-worth. Through raw vulnerability and unwavering faith, she reveals how even life's greatest struggles can shape us into vessels of healing and purpose. Her mission is a guiding light, inspiring us to embrace who we are and lead with courage, resilience, and impact.
— **Lauren Sisler**, ESPN reporter, motivational speaker, author of *Shatterproof*

In *Finding My Course*, Tracy Hanson invites the reader to join her on a purposeful journey that will do more than pique their interest; it will change their lives. She courageously shares her life story of success, failure, regret, and trauma, unveiling the pathway she discovered that will inspire us to rise from life's bunkers to the victor's podium. I highly recommend this book to everyone who desires to live a life that is anything but par for the course.
— **Jay Mills**, former NCAA D1 head football coach, author, speaker, and founder of CJM Ministries

Tracy Hanson is a woman known for her courage, tenacity, drive, and love of chocolate chip cookies. The story of how she came to be a professional athlete is inspiring, and the deeper story of how she recovered her own heart is stunning.
— **Tracy Johnson**, ReStory Counseling Storywork Supervisor; founder, Red Tent Living

A PROFESSIONAL ATHLETE'S
JOURNEY THROUGH PAIN TO PURPOSE

FINDING MY COURSE

TRACY HANSON

Finding My Course: A Professional Athlete's Journey Through Pain to Purpose
Copyright © 2025 by Tracy Hanson

tracyhanson.com/

Published by Do Good Books
Gilbert, Arizona
dogoodbooks.com/

ISBN 978-0-9712723-8-5

All rights reserved. No portion of this book may be used or reproduced, stored in a retrieval system, or transmitted in any form or by any means—electronic, mechanical, photocopying, recording, scanning, or other—except for brief quotations in critical reviews of articles, without the prior written permission of the publisher.

Unless otherwise marked, all scripture quotations are from the Holy Bible, English Standard Version®, copyright © 2001 by Crossway, a publishing ministry of Good News Publishers. Used by permission. All rights reserved. ESV Text Edition: 2011

Scripture quotations marked NIV are from the Holy Bible, New International Version®, NIV®. Copyright 1973, 1978, 1984, 2011 by Biblica, Inc. ® Used by permission of Zondervan. All rights reserved worldwide. www.Zondervan.com

Collaborative Writer: Lauren Befus
Copy Editor: Chris Gettle
Developmental Editor/Book Coach: Anita K. Palmer
Cover and Interior Design: Kate Hoyman, Design9Studios
Cover Photo: Rich Heins. © Rich Heins Photography. Used by permission.

Published in the United States of America

For Haley, Courtney, and André

TABLE OF CONTENTS

Dedication — iii
Table of Contents — v
Foreword — ix
Introduction — xi

Part One: The Before

1 // IT'S A GIRL — 3
2 // THE BURGER GAME — 5
3 // EXPLORERS EXTRAORDINAIRE — 6
4 // BEYOND OUR BACKYARDS — 8
5 // MY FIRST BAD SWING — 10
6 // UNPACKING ANGER IN TLV — 11
7 // ELEMENTARY SCHOOL WHISPERS — 13
8 // SHOPPING WITH A TOMBOY — 14
9 // MY PARENTS — 16
10 // HER EYES — 18
11 // CHOCOLATE CHIP COOKIES — 20
12 // FIGHT THE GIRL — 21
13 // GOLF WITH MY DAD — 23
14 // MY FIRST 9-HOLE TOURNAMENT — 25
15 // DAD'S ATTENTION — 27
16 // THE TRUNK — 28
17 // A SIXTH-GRADE FIELD DAY — 30
18 // SWINGING THROUGH THE SUMMERS — 31
19 // THE SUMMER SCHEDULE — 33
20 // STERN AND LOVING HEARTS — 36
21 // VROOM VROOM — 38
22 // DRIBBLING TO SUCCESS — 40
23 // INTRO TO JESUS — 42
24 // THE FORD ESCORT — 44

25 // BOYFRIENDS — 46
26 // STUCK UP — 48
27 // MAKING VARSITY — 51
28 // SCOOTER AND SHAGGY — 52
29 // "I JUST CAN'T" — 54
30 // HIGH-PRESSURE GOLF — 55

Part Two: The During

31 // SPECIAL TREATMENT — 61
32 // "IT'S COACH TO YOU" — 63
33 // HOME VISITS — 65
34 // WE WON — 66
35 // COLLEGE VISITS — 68
36 // DINNER ALONE — 71
37 // IT'S OKAY — 73
38 // MY CADDY — 75
39 // ALMOST — 79
40 // DON'T LEAVE — 81
41 // EVERYTHING IS OKAY — 83
42 // A NEW ERA — 86
43 // UNTRACEABLE — 89
44 // DISTRACTIONS — 90
45 // TREMORS — 93
46 // ENDING IT — 95
47 // ASKING FORGIVENESS — 97

Part Three: The Aftermath

48 // BREAKING 70 — 103
49 // HOME FOR SUMMER — 105
50 // THE NEXT STEP — 107
51 // A YEAR OF FIRSTS — 110
52 // A SUMMER OF SUCCESS — 112
53 // A DIRT DARE — 114
54 // UPS AND DOWNS — 115

55 // UNDER PRESSURE	119
56 // A VICODIN-INDUCED FOG	120
57 // POMP AND CIRCUMSTANCE	124
58 // A QUICK TRIP	126
59 // MY JOB IS REHAB	127
60 // TWO DIFFERENT PEOPLE	129

Part Four: The After

61 // Q-SCHOOL TAKE ONE	135
62 // A NEW PLAN	139
63 // Q-SCHOOL TAKE TWO	141
64 // ROOKIE OF THE YEAR … ALMOST	143
65 // FELLOWSHIP	146
66 // AFTER-HOURS ADVENTURES	149
67 // GRIMY HOTELS AND PRIVATE HOUSING	151
68 // SIXTY-THREE: A CAREER BEST	153
69 // THIS TIME?	155
70 // TRAVEL WARS	157
71 // ALONE AGAIN	161
72 // NO MERCY	162
73 // A ROUND WITH NANCY LOPEZ	165
74 // THE JUNIOR CLINIC	167
75 // THE WORLD IS SPINNING	168
76 // A SPECIAL VISITOR	171
77 // THE LAST TIME	174
78 // MOM'S LAST WORDS	175
79 // BOUND TO THE LIE	177
80 // ASK AND YOU WILL RECEIVE	178
81 // NEW LIFE	180
82 // NATIONAL TRAGEDY	181
83 // NOW THERE ARE TWO	184
84 // THREE?	185
85 // LOSING SHELI	186
86 // ON-COURSE ANTICS	188

87 // CHILLED TO THE BONE	191
88 // ADVERSITY AND GRIT	193
89 // GOLF NIGHTMARES	196
90 // CADDIES	198
91 // A NECESSARY ENDING	202
92 // BROKEN ENGAGEMENT	204
93 // NAMING SEXUAL ABUSE	206
94 // AN END AT CORNING	209
95 // FRONT ROW AGAIN	211
96 // A NEW ROUTINE	213

Part Five: The Healing

97 // THE BLINK OF AN EYE	221
98 // NAMING TRUTH	223
99 // A YEAR OF GROWTH	225
100 // GROUP WORK	226
101 // ALONE AGAIN	229
102 // KENYA	231
103 // RECOVERY WEEK	234
104 // NEW KIND OF TRAINING	237
105 // COAT OF ARMS	240
106 // OUT OF THE ROUGH	243
107 // THE CROSSROADS	245
108 // WHERE GOLF AND LIFE COLLIDE	247
109 // MY "WHY" IS WORTH IT	249

Appendix A: Notes to Athletes, Families, and Coaches	253
Appendix B: "Why Jesus?"	256
Appendix C: "For Mom"	258
Appendix D: A Glossary for Non-Golfers	259
Acknowledgments	261
About the Author	263
About the Tracy Hanson Initiative	264

FOREWORD

Does the Gospel have anything to say to broken people who live life in silence because of some past harm perpetrated on them by others? Who believe they participated in the behavior, and therefore they are to blame? Do they need to prove every day that they are good enough for God—to "perform" to be worthy of his love? If they're Christians and/or church-goers, is church a place where they have to hide behind a false veneer of perfection to stay "safe" around other Christians?

These questions are important for the worldwide faith community in general, and to so many of us personally today. But they hit home especially hard for victims of sexual abuse, and even harder for victims of trauma who use victory in elite sports to self-medicate their pain, and harder still for those who add living on a treadmill of earning God's approval as the false answer for all their other problems.

Tracy Hanson knows these tensions all too well: a survivor of emotional abandonment as a child; a teenage victim of sexual abuse from a trusted, crucially influential individual; and a member of the LPGA for fifteen seasons, who tried to win the approval of others (and of herself) through success in golf, while seeking at the same time to gain God's acceptance by her Christian witness as a professional.

Tracy tells her story with heart-breaking honesty, page-turning prose, and hard-won wisdom. As a result, she gives the reader a ring-side seat to watch God and his Gospel over time work his freeing truth deep inside her. Little by little, God helps Tracy realize that she is not defined by her accomplishments, as impressive as they are, nor by the failure of others towards her, as devastating as they were, nor even by her own frailties, as persistent as they remain still today.

Rather, Tracy has come to embrace more and more each day that Christ's unconditional love has given her a worth and value that she couldn't earn and now can never lose.

When Tracy ends her book by telling of the work of the Tracy Hanson

Initiative today, the reader, like Tracy, is confident that God will bring to completion the good work that has begun in the lives of many elite athletes today, because he is doing that in and through his handiwork in Tracy.

—The Rt. Rev. Canon Dr. John Ashley Null,
Bishop of the Anglican Diocese of North Africa;
Chair, Wittenberg [Germany] Center for Reformation Studies;
and Olympic and Elite Sports Chaplain

INTRODUCTION

I push the gear shift into park and exhale before opening the door. The climb up the alley of stairs to Kay's condo is a familiar trek by now. Where she wants to take me, however, has my stomach tied up in knots.

The 2011 summer season is just getting underway at Maranatha, a huge retreat and conference center in the township of Norton Shores, Michigan. From late June to Labor Day, hundreds of people come to enjoy Lake Michigan and attend daily Bible teaching. Each week representatives from a different global mission group also are on campus to share what their ministry is doing. Kay has invited me to come to Maranatha to meet one of the female leaders from the group currently on campus.

After the short walk from the condo to the meeting in the Skinner Room, Kay opens the door and my feet follow. The rest of me tightens. My eyes dart around the room of fifty or so people, looking for a way to escape. The low ceiling makes the room feel claustrophobic. Thankfully, Kay suggests we sit in the back row. I release another breath trapped in my throat and sit before anyone could say hello.

The hour presentation feels like an eternity. I examine the speakers. Which one will I meet?

When the presentation is done, I hang behind Kay. She side-steps and introduces me to a woman. Coincidentally, she's also named Tracy. Sounds crossed my ear drums, but I hear only gibberish.

"We are going to join Tracy in the snack shop for lunch in about fifteen minutes."

"OK," I say, holding my breath again.

Once I've made my way to the camp's little cafe, my food sits in front of me untouched. I answer a few questions that Tracy asks. Then it all erupts.

Tears. More tears. Snot. And more tears.

I vomit words I had never spoken out loud before. Tracy and Kay's compassion and kindness envelop me. I'm thirty-nine years old and this is the first time I feel like someone finally heard the cry of my heart.

In the following pages is the story I discovered after I asked for help.

PART ONE:
THE BEFORE

1 // IT'S A GIRL

I slid rapidly into the cold hospital room in Coeur d'Alene, Idaho, at 10:18 am, October 28, 1971. Fathers still weren't allowed into some labor rooms in this era, so Mom was alone. My dad, Thomas Arthur Hanson, waited somewhere in the recesses of the hospital halls.

The anticipation of a boy entering the family was high. After two girls under his wing, my dad wanted a boy. With no power over such an expectation, Mom at least agreed to the boy's name he picked out. Troy Arthur Hanson was ready for the birth certificate. This baby would be the last hope for the Hanson namesake to be carried on.

My bald head and striking blue eyes encapsulated the Hanson Norwegian genes. But my gender would be the end of the family line. With no girl's name on the list, my mom asked Colleen English, her best friend, about using the girl's name Colleen had never used due to having only boys. I do think my mom liked the name Tracy Ann, and it would satisfy the pursuit of a name that still gave me my dad's initials: T.A.H. At this juncture of life, I have no way of knowing, I will just say that Mom had Colleen's blessings to name me Tracy Ann Hanson.

I'm not sure what happens in the hours or days after a baby enters the world. But something got muddled up in the signing of my birth certificate. The story I have been carrying most of my life goes like this.

When the nurse handed Mom the birth certificate, she quickly signed it without noticing that the spelling of my name was Tracie instead of Tracy. Frustrated and deflated by the mistake, Mom reluctantly accepted the claim that only the court system could change it and my name would forever be Tracie Ann Hanson.

The spelling didn't change the fact that I was a girl and not a boy. My dad waded through his disappointment as best he could. Pictures portray his playfulness with me early on, and I was his namesake for better or worse.

Blond, wispy locks finally grew out to my little shoulders and baby dresses clothed me. But something was shifting as I turned three. By age four, my hair was cut shorter, and the dresses disappeared. I don't know all the forces at play, but my looks and interests turned toward what the boys were doing. I slid into my tomboy years full force—to my dad's delight.

Meanwhile, after three years of writing *Tracie* on my birthday cakes, Mom's angst about the birth certificate debacle broke through the locked door it had been hidden behind. On July 29, 1974, Mom, with paperwork in hand, walked into the Kootenai County Courthouse, resolved to claim her wish to change the spelling of my name by the Idaho State Registrar of Vital Statistics. Who knew that a name was a vital statistic?

It's funny how a simple change of spelling makes me proud of my name. I love that Mom took the initiative for her and for me. Her stubbornness to stand up for what she wanted (not something I often witnessed during my childhood years) lives in me. It's hard to know what Mom was feeling when she walked into that courthouse to file the paperwork. But for me, I embody her defiance and ownership in my namesake. I love my name, *Tracy*—with a Y.

2 // THE BURGER GAME

Despite their different temperaments, Colleen and my mom were close. They parented the four of us kids (Todd and Eric English; my older sister Debbie and me) together. Living within walking distance of one another, so much life was shared—recipes, meals, playdates, and commiserating over parenting. Even a pottery business was born and shared between the two women.

The six of us often drove the thirty minutes across the valley into Spokane, Washington, to visit the shops connected via skywalks downtown or to play along the river park. Stopping at our lunchtime favorite—McDonald's—was also a norm. Fellow kindergartener Eric and I, eager to prove we were big kids, claimed a table for the kids and shooed our mothers off to a table of their own. They were more than willing to oblige.

Eric and I ordered our usual—a hamburger, fries, and a milkshake. Our big kid status quickly disintegrated when we decided to invent a highly acclaimed game only the greatest minds could understand.

The game's rules:

1. Stuff as much of your burger into your mouth as you could.
2. Determine who ate their burger in the fewest bites.
3. Commence a burping contest.

Todd and Debbie flushed red and pleaded with our mothers to make us stop. But our moms pretended they didn't know who we belonged to. They simply unleashed the patented "mom evil eye" and silence descended.

Usually, Eric won in two bites. With all my might, I tried to stuff that hamburger in my mouth, but I routinely secured second place with three bites.

3 // EXPLORERS EXTRAORDINAIRE

I was one of the boys, at least with Eric and Todd. Our Post Falls, Idaho, neighborhood held a feast of wonders, and it was up to us, young explorers, to find them. We searched for snakes and frogs, experimented with mud pies, and hiked the treacherous mountain road to seek out treasure. (Really, a large hill down to Gish's Corner gas station to buy candy.) Sometimes Debbie joined in too. In our little world, we reigned. Nothing could overrule us or keep us from our expeditions.

Including school. To our dismay, we made it out of kindergarten and started first grade. It was 1977 and Eric had already turned six; I was still five until October.

Seltice Elementary School hunkered close to the ground and gloomed over the children every morning. Eric and I trudged off the bus one day and lingered in the schoolyard. We glanced at our first-grade classmates falling in line, then out to the distance, where the marvel of the railroad tracks beckoned us.

After all, the two of us had a history. We both had tested high and had low patience for sitting around. I refused to take naps and got bored. We were always getting into trouble. Colleen, Eric's mother, had to beg the kindergarten teacher to let him return to class after being kicked out. Miss Eileen was more than ready to graduate us to first grade.

Soon enough, we embarked on another quest—a mile down the tracks to the Handy Mart. We frolicked in our perceived freedom that morning, away from the drudgery of the classroom, away from the lines, away into adventure.

Eventually, we returned, in time for recess. The bell rang. We fell into line. The teachers didn't yell at us or question our arrival. We spent the rest of the afternoon in class. At the end of the day, we rode the bus home with Debbie, my older sister, and Todd. Nothing had changed. Or so we thought.

It was the perfect day.

Eric and Todd split off to their home several houses down, ready to watch *The Flintstones* and munch on after-school snacks, while Debbie and I did the same back at our house. All appeared normal.

Colleen greeted the boys. "Did you do anything interesting today?"

Todd, knowing nothing of our escapade, said "Nope."

"You know?" Eric sheepishly blurted, seeing *the look* in his mother's eyes.

"Know what?"

"About Tracy and me?"

"Yes, Eric. Mothers have eyes in the back of their heads. We see everything and we know everything."

Colleen knew from the beginning. A teacher's aide spied us when she arrived late to work that morning. She called Colleen, who laughed and told her to not bother us but to call if we didn't come back by recess. (These were the days when kids could roam in Northern Idaho without much worry about safety.) Colleen activated her own network of spies, asking others to keep an eye on us around town. Knowing my mom might not see the situation as lightly, she asked the school not to call her.

When we arrived back at school, the teacher's aide called Colleen back, informing her the two wayward delinquents had returned. Everyone but my mother knew.

Colleen sternly told Eric, "If you do it again, there will be hell to pay." Before telling my mom about our escapade, Colleen gave me the same talking to, hoping it would lessen the heat my mom would feel toward me.

I honestly don't remember my mom's response. I could have been grounded or given a spanking with the dreaded stick. Both happened often to try and tame my strong-willed spirit.

Eric and I never skipped school again. But it wasn't the last trouble we stirred.

4 // BEYOND OUR BACKYARDS

Eric and I continued our antics and explorations beyond our hometown of Post Falls during family vacations spent together from 1975 to around 1981. For as long as I can remember, our childhood spring break trips unfolded in Vantage, Washington, with camping and riding motorcycles through the sand dunes just east of the mighty Columbia River that wound through that dry basin. Multiple families joined us setting up our group site. For an entire week, moms, dads, girls, boys, and animals created a playground out of those dunes. We rode across them each day, dirt and dust clinging to our bodies.

On one of our early trips to Vantage, Eric and I explored the campsite, assessing the familiar RVs circled around the fire pit. The older kids had disappeared to who knows where. Alone, Eric and I (the youngest in the camp) surveyed the scene—the adults in scattered groups playing cards or chatting; their empty beer cans strewn about the camp. Eric led the vanguard; I kept the rear. Our mission objective: to retrieve the *near* empty beer cans. Soon enough, we touched back on our homebase, the English family van where we quickly disposed of the beer by drinking it, backwash and all.

Then the van doors opened. Our horrified mothers glared at us, two best friends and drunk troublemakers, giggling and dancing the night away.

From the very beginning, motorcycles were a part of my world. In an old photograph I'm perched on my dad's HONDA. An oversized helmet wobbles on my head. I beam from my spot, the oval, white-framed sunglasses shielding my eyes. I sat mostly on the gray gas tank, my backside barely touching the worn leather seat. My father sits behind me, holding up the motorcycle and intently looking at me to prevent my younger than two-year-old self from toppling over.

I cannot remember this moment, but the photograph remains, and illustrates how my love for motorcycles began before I can remember. Both my parents rode. Mom usually had Debbie with her while I smiled with glee in front of Dad. I'm not sure how much Mom enjoyed the rides, but there we were, a family of four saddled up to enjoy the open road.

At the age of four, I received the green light to ride our family's fat-wheeled mono-bike. I wanted to ride with the boys, to go on a sand-dune adventure of my own. I was determined to conquer the beast. The mono-bike only had one speed and weighed as much as a heavy bicycle. Balancing was tricky. When the motor lit, the mono-bike became a machine with a mind of its own. My dad guided me and watched me get the hang of it. He ran alongside me as I bounced down the dirt path, a hand on the bike until he released me. One second, two seconds, all on my own.

Then, it all unraveled.

My vocabulary did not contain the phrase, "fight, flight or freeze response," but my body responded in full force. I froze, my right hand on the open throttle. The frame beneath me cut and swerved. *Left. Right. Up. Down.* My body catapulted into the thick of a thorny tumbleweed bush. I lay in shock, until my dad reached me. When I saw him, my wailing erupted.

The tears and dust formed a dirty paste on my cheeks as Mom plucked the thorns out of me and my clothes. My courage rebounded, though, and I was ready to try again. Each time I crashed, I got back up and tried again. Nothing was going to stop me. At the end of the day, covered from head to toe in dirt, a proud mono-biker returned to the campsite able to ride the mono-bike all by herself.

I soon graduated to a real bike with gears, a snappy Honda 50, painted red with brown decals. I felt so big on that bike. I rode it up and over the small dunes, and back at home all over the wooded expanse that surrounded our house in Post Falls. The boys in the neighborhood and I created our own trails, pretended we were racing, and rode for hours.

That same summer when I was five, I rode the Honda in the local Fourth of July parade. The year before, I was stuck on top of the Kiwanis float, forced to wear a dress. My outfit on my motorcycle was a complete one-eighty from that dress. I dazzled the crowd with my cowboy jeans and hat, bandanna, and my plastic rifle stashed in a holster attached to the left side of my bike. I felt large, proud, and important.

5 // MY FIRST BAD SWING

I was only five years old when I first laid eyes on a golf club. Billy, the oldest among us neighbor kids, came out of his garage holding one and I was immediately intrigued. Basketball, baseball, football—those were sports I was familiar with. But golf? This was new.

After watching Billy swing at the grass a few times, somehow the club found its way into my tiny hands. Not to be outdone by the boys, and without warning, I set a swing in motion with all the strength my little body could muster. In my haste to impress, I failed to consider who was within range of my mighty stroke until the stick in my hand stopped suddenly with a big thud.

Alarmed, I turned around just in time to see blood wash over Billy's face from an unidentified spot. My feet barely held my numb body as the words disappeared in my throat. The gushing blood painted the grass. An air raid of screams called into the house for help.

Within moments, Billy's mom cradled him in her arms and into the car; tail lights speeding away toward the hospital.

The club missed Billy's eyeball by millimeters. My body still shudders as I remember the event. My excitement to show off to everyone turned into a nightmare. Stunned and scared, my insides went cold and numb. *I am bad. I hurt my friend.*

Before life returned to normal, my dad announced we would be moving.

Part One: The Before

6 // UNPACKING ANGER IN TLV

It was 1977 and we were driving away from the best childhood home on Royal Highlands in Post Falls I ever knew. I wish I remembered every precise detail. My world was coming to an end, and I was only six.

Mom, Debbie, and I were tucked into the station wagon, our silence enveloping our anger and sadness. Mom didn't want to move away from Colleen. I belonged at Royal Highlands with my playmates. Debbie was sad to leave the Englishes and scared to start a new school. Turning the corner to head down the hill, my insides felt like they were going to explode. We veered north to cross the prairie, a seven-mile stretch of grassland. The only world I knew blurred through my tears and quiet sobs.

We moved a dozen miles to Twin Lakes Village, or TLV as it was often called, weeks before I started second grade. The nine-hole golf course community felt like a different country. In Post Falls, our house looked out over the prairie. I loved that view, even as a young child. After my traumatic experience nearly gouging out an eye, I surely wasn't interested in golf either. In TLV, I lived in a duplex half the size of my old house. Pine trees enveloped our new home but parted enough to give us a view of the par-3 hole 5 at the edge of the course property.

My new space didn't feel like home. Rigidity and fear kept me company, fretting over nightmares in which King Kong chased me into darkness. Back on the south side of the prairie in Post Falls, I experienced normal friction that occurs among kids, and while I tested my parents' boundaries, I loved my little life. But in TLV, my simmering anger began to ooze. Fury for leaving behind the Englishes (Bruce, Colleen, Todd, and Eric) and the familiarity. I saw nothing but a gloomy unknown ahead. That unknown included a new school at the end of a four-mile bus ride.

I trapped my big feelings away in my small body. Sometimes, they found their way out, turning me into a tornado. My parents reacted with spankings and sent me to my room, rarely asking me how I felt. At the height of one of my explosions, I screamed at Mom that I was going to run away. I grabbed some belongings from my room, sped down the stairs, and barreled toward the front door. Mom opened it for me—and warned me my father would be home soon.

I ran out. As if on cue, my father pulled into the driveway.

I froze on the steps. His words still ring through my head today, "If you ever try to run away again, I will hang you up in the garage by your coat."

I don't believe he would have done it, but his words scared the hell out of me. I returned to my room, and my anger settled into the recesses of my soul.

Time crawled along, and I came to terms with living in TLV. Dad built us a house on the ninth hole, away from the pine trees of the course's back corner. The fairway out back appeared to be a wide-open space, but it was not the view of the sprawling prairie from Royal Highlands in Post Falls.

7 // ELEMENTARY SCHOOL WHISPERS

I shuffled through the empty, quiet school hallway toward the bathroom. The lockers blurred on both sides of my vision. I pushed my seven-year-old frame against the bathroom's steel door, its coolness surprising me.

The bathroom looked like every other school bathroom, with cinder-block and a pasty gray hue. Once through the door, I turned right. My gaze came up from the floor and met the eyes of another girl. She froze for an eternity, staring at me until she ran past and threw open the steel door.

"There's a boy in the girls' bathroom!"

Her screams echoed down the empty hallway and drifted into the bathroom. My body flooded with shock, and I felt cold. I can't recall if I ended up even using the toilet.

I shuffled back to the classroom. I pushed open the door, and time slowed to a standstill. More than twenty sets of eyes stared back at me. The blood drained out of my face and my eyes dropped to the tile floor beneath my feet.

I turned my head back toward the door, wanting to flee, but our teacher broke the silence and asked me to return to my seat. Yet, my heart heard the whispers. Whispers from the kids at my new school. Whispers from the evil one. The lies penetrated deep until they felt true—I was different; I didn't belong.

8 // SHOPPING WITH A TOMBOY

I darted under racks of clothes in the boys' section and prepared myself for battle. My mom dragged me out fighting and screaming, her hand gripping my upper arm. I mustered up every inch of resistance I could, and she led me toward the girls' section by any means possible. Pushing, forcing, dragging—she used all the methods in her playbook. But the moment she released her hand from my arm, I scurried back to the safety of my hiding place to prepare myself for Round Two of the fight.

I marvel at myself in old photos. I see a feisty, bright-eyed girl exploring her world with wonder. In my second year of life, my bald head turned into wispy locks of blond hair barely brushing my shoulders. My wardrobe consisted mainly of cute, tiny baby dresses and tights.

Then something happened. Between my third and fourth birthdays, a sudden shift occurred. A bowl-cut replaced my shoulder-length hair. The dresses ceased abruptly. I wanted to dress like Eric, Todd, and the other boys in our neighborhood. I was one of them, after all. We mixed mud pies, climbed trees, and foraged in the woods on foot and on our Honda 50 motorcycles. Our daily activities required a standard uniform of T-shirts and jeans. My frilly dresses and other girly clothes slowly disappeared from my drawers to be replaced with outdoor play wear.

I even wanted to pee standing up like the neighborhood boys did. *Why couldn't I?* My mother gave me a multitude of reasons why not and swiftly put a stop to my bathroom antics.

On Christmas Day when I was five, my giant grin—minus my front teeth—spread my cheeks and made my eyes squint. I could barely contain my excitement over my gifts, including a Rams football jersey, a football helmet, and a yellow Tonka Truck. The helmet wobbled on my shoulders, and the oversized jersey draped to my knees. The mighty dump truck's bucket moved up and down. I couldn't wait to show the English boys my new toy. In my five-year-old wisdom, I declared it the best Christmas Day ever.

Every year, we shopped at the local Woolworth's for back-to-school clothes. My sister Debbie was easy. She picked out blouses, dresses, and jeans, tried them on, and danced out of the store joyfully. Me? Not so much. Shopping only reminded me of how different I felt. To this day, I hate shopping.

One year, my poor mother was so frustrated, embarrassed, and depleted of all resolve that one of the saleswomen, a friend of hers, offered to help me shop while my mom left the store. The saleswoman negotiated a compromise. I begrudgingly assented to a few items off the girl's rack, but absolutely no dress.

Eventually, Mom surrendered and let me select the clothes I wanted.

Later, we switched our shopping destination to downtown Spokane, where we walked above ground level between shops via the sky walks. I refused to enter a single store until Mom promised me a dozen Great American Cookie Company's mini chocolate chip cookies. She reluctantly obliged and sent me on the route with cash in my hands. Another battle, another win.

9 // MY PARENTS

Early images of my mother, Marcella Louise, show her eyes bright with excitement. She was my grandmother Lorraine's firstborn—a lively little girl growing up in the northwest corner of Washington State.

Before my mom reached her fourth birthday, her father skipped out on the family. Devastated, my grandmother's only choice—to divorce this man—resulted in the Roman Catholic Church promptly excommunicating her and her children. There was no care or concern for the well-being of the humans left in the wreckage. Mom never talked about those years. The unmentionable pain was packed neatly away forever.

The grandfather I grew up with, Earl Carroll, came into the picture a couple of years later. A United States Coast Guard Chief Petty Officer, E-9 rank, an engine mechanic, he adopted my mom and her younger brother, Eddie, before she turned seven. I would come to know him as PāPā.

PāPā ruled as the harsh military head of the family. Wherever he was posted for the Coast Guard, they followed. They went as far as Hawaii to the west, Boston to the east, and Alaska to the north. My mom rarely shared memories, good or bad, but her face lit up with joy when she described exploring the Honolulu banyan trees in bare feet.

A decade later, she was sexually abused by a family member. Instead of the perpetrator being exposed, it was Mom who suffered the consequences. With packed bags, she traveled thousands of miles away from her home to live with family friends in California. Not too long after, Mom met and married a military man to escape California, and her heartache.

As one trauma tends to follow another, less than a year into marriage, this man's abuse forced my mom to divorce him. Mom made her way to a friend in North Idaho to start over again.

With her flipped brunette hairstyle and striking face, Mom found a job as a bank teller. Here into the story enters my future father, the manager of this regional bank office.

Tom Hanson was an Idaho native. Generations had been born and raised in Coeur d'Alene. Dad's childhood was tumultuous at best. His mom, my paternal grandmother, divorced my grandfather and moved to the west side of Washington State when Dad was young. She left Dad in Idaho; he was mostly raised by his grandparents and his alcoholic father, whom I never knew. I was told that Dad's father held me in infancy but died before I was one year old.

Dad's social personality escorted him through high school (a trait my two sisters inherited). He was an average athlete, more known for his trumpet skills.

I don't know what attracted my parents to each other. Did Dad's charisma draw Marcella out? Did he eloquently paint a mirage in which her traumatized soul sought refuge? For by no means were all of his intentions pure.

Pregnancy led to marriage and my sister was born. Eighteen months later, I completed the family unit. We also had an older half-sister, Sheli, from Dad's previous marriage that had ended in disaster due to his infidelity. We didn't see Sheli as much as we wanted to. I wouldn't find out until after my mother died—when I was twenty-six—that Dad also had an affair while Mom was pregnant with me. Heartbroken but with one divorce already in her story, she chose to stay.

Mom and Dad always showed up for golf tournaments and all my basketball games and band concerts. To an outside observer, they appeared to be a happy middle-class couple. My sister remembers screaming fights behind closed doors, but I don't. The sporadically loud bursts of anger between them were followed quickly with Mom numbing into quiet, while he disappeared into his Bud Light.

10 // HER EYES

Our eyes lock and my toddler arms squeeze against my body as I reach out to imitate my mom's hands curled into fists in front of me. Giggles erupt from my belly. Our play-boxing hits nothing but air. Mom's eyes rebound the little squeals of delight.

Mom loved to be with her girls. Whether outside or in, she enjoyed playing with us. During Christmas and spring breaks, she rode motorcycles, snowmobiled, and downhill skied alongside Dad, Debbie, and me.

There was something about my mother's eyes. They expressed lightness and ease. Even when my eyes were swollen with rebellion, Mom's could still get through to me. Her eyes betrayed her unspoken emotions, revealing the unsaid. My mom's nature was to be quiet yet opinionated with a twist of sarcasm on top.

While she worked outside the home, Mom was still accessible and home after school. Mom wasn't an extravagant cook. We mostly lived off the stockpile of Schwan's dinners in the freezer. She always had something ready to be reheated when sports took over our schedules. Sometimes, though, she made her sweet spaghetti sauce and a mouthwatering chili with cornbread.

At bedtime, she always said, "I love you." Her physical presence was consistent, but after the move to TLV, I don't remember snuggling up to her while she read me a book. I don't recall any soft conversations, any deep examinations into how I was really doing. TLV had taken Mom away from her best friend and all that was familiar. Mom's emotional well had run dry.

Around when I was nine, Mom had major surgery and from that point on I made my own lunches for school. In the years following, she stopped playing with us and participating in our outdoor adventures on school breaks. She would work part of the time and face more illness. Books were her companions, exploring romance novels and the imaginary worlds of science fiction.

Yet, Mom loved to travel in the real world, too. Both parents attended my youth golf tournaments in the Pacific Northwest, St. Louis, and Florida, but it was my mom who ventured farther. She loved the experiences and traveling also allowed her to escape the loneliness she felt at home. When I was eleven, she drove me to San Diego to play the World Junior Championship held on the world-famous Torrey Pines Golf Course, and she flew to my first USGA Junior Girls Championship in South Hadley, Massachusetts.

As my junior and high school years passed, Mom drifted inward while Dad lost himself in work and the local pubs. The reality of their transactional relationship culminated during my mom's fight with melanoma. I was a pro on the LPGA Tour when she reached the late stages. As cancer ravaged her body, her eyes became vacant. After she died, my dreams for many years would be haunted by those eyes.

11 // CHOCOLATE CHIP COOKIES

I'm not usually big on old movies. But if there's one I get nostalgic about, it's the 1958 film *South Pacific*. That's what was playing one snowy Saturday afternoon in 1980 when Mom and I were home together baking chocolate chip cookies. Our TV was nestled high in the brick wall of the family room and we had a direct view of it from the kitchen. I can almost still see tropical scenes dancing across the screen and hear the songs playing in my mind.

I wasn't captivated by the wartime romance musical so much as I was about getting to bake with Mom.

Her cookie recipe went something like this:

Measure out the dry ingredients—flour, salt, and baking soda—and mix them in a small bowl. In a large bowl, beat the wet ingredients—butter, white sugar, brown sugar, vanilla, and eggs. Slowly add the dry mix to the wet mix, folding with a spatula until just combined. Then, add an entire bag of chocolate chips. Except, Mom always ate more than one spoonful of dough before adding the chips. She loved chocolate chip cookies *minus* the chocolate. I never did understand that about her.

With my ability to manage the ingredients on my own, and to carefully stir the dough, Mom's involvement decreased in the process. But she continued to sneak a chocolate chip-less dough ball or two when I wasn't looking.

I never met a chocolate morsel I didn't like. Just the smell of baking cookies takes me back to that day—the day I fell in love with chocolate chip cookies. As *South Pacific* played, snow covered the golf course in our backyard, and Mom and I made memories in the kitchen.

A warm, gooey chocolate chip cookie is still one of my favorite things. It brings back a warm, fuzzy memory and making cookie dough has been a source of comfort for me. To this day I smile thinking of Mom sneaking bites of the dough before I added in the chocolate chips. Since Mom's death, every time I make cookies, I feel her with me.

12 // FIGHT THE GIRL

I stared down Chris, one of the strongest boys in our fourth-grade class. I had no chance but I wasn't one to back down from a fight. Our playground antics had somehow evolved into a wrestling match. As we thrashed on the ground together, I grunted and heaved, struggling against him to no avail. Then, an opening appeared. I delivered a swift kick to his face.

Chris immediately let go and cupped his oozing, bloody lip. I squirmed backward, putting distance between us. Adrenaline coursed through my body.

Over the next six years Chris and I would develop a cat-and-mouse friendship. By the time we were seniors, we chose to walk into commencement together.

My tomboy identity ran deep. I was a tough girl with nothing "girly" about me. I played football and other games with the boys during each recess. I tended to be mostly quiet in class. In third grade, I had suffered an embarrassing speech impediment. It was gone now, but I hid my insecurity behind my tough-girl act. That was my safe place, and I remained quiet—unless provoked.

Fifth grade was in a new school building, a historic monolith with mountainous cement stairs. We had a homeroom, but for the first time, we changed classrooms a few times a day, moving throughout the school, up and down the different floors.

One gray otherwise uneventful day, we all twitched with antsy energy, ready for recess. The electricity mounted when a girl called me a name in front of everyone in class. My face flushed with embarrassment, my little body hot with rage.

I instantly retaliated, "I'll meet you on the playground."

As the school ran out for recess, our class huddled at the bottom of the stairs. I was ready for my opponent, primed from schoolyard wrestling matches. She cowered before me, her face lined with fear. It didn't matter to me. My anger unleashed and, with one swing across her fearful face, she hit the ground.

The crowd spotted a teacher and quickly scattered. The girl stood as the teacher approached. I glared at her, forcing her into silence. She told the teacher she tripped, too scared of the teacher's wrath and mine.

Puberty came for me in sixth grade. I started to feel different. The bowl haircut my dad encouraged me to wear began to bother me. I felt new things when a boy passed a note my way. As my puberty hormones raged, new battle lines for my femininity were drawn inside me.

Sixth grade is an awkward and distressing time for any kid. I forged through the muck of my adolescence, trying to figure out who I was. One day I decided to wear a dress, a self-inflicted test against my awkward non-girly-ness. I had never worn a dress to school. It felt risky and new to display a different facet of myself to my classmates.

The familiar schoolyard blurred as I stepped off the school bus. I dug deep for every ounce of courage as my toe touched the concrete sidewalk. My classmates stared. My brain morphed their stares into ridicule, words they never spoke, but I heard all the same.

My attempt at wearing a dress backfired. I felt like a fraud. I didn't feel like a real girl. That day, I made a vow that I would never wear a dress again.

13 // GOLF WITH MY DAD

With my anger toward moving to TLV beginning to thaw during our second year at the townhouse, my curiosity for the par-3 across the street, a hole a seasoned golfer is expected to need only three strokes to finish—one stroke to get the ball on the green, followed by two putts—began to bloom.

When Dad was available some summer evenings in those years, from 1978 to around 1980, we would saunter over and hit balls down the little hole over and over. He showed me how to hold the club and take a basic back and through swing. Mostly, I wanted to swing as hard as I could all the time.

My natural athleticism took to golf quickly. This didn't mean my swing came together with ease or my first scores broke any early records. I caught the bug, though, and dropped playing softball to focus on golf.

I borrowed Mom's clubs, which she rarely used. That gave her a good excuse for why she couldn't play (she really had little interest in golf). I was proud of her PowerBilt clubs, the set that helped me get started and play my first year of tournaments.

My dad passed me off to our local club pro for lessons soon after I showed a committed interest around age nine. That was one of his better decisions, since he was barely an average golfer himself and knew little about the golf swing. However, that didn't stop him from trying to help me along the way (if you can call it help).

My desire to have fun with my dad always seemed to sour on the golf course. He poked my sleeping anger. Instead of encouraging and helping regulate my frustrations, he needled and stirred up my temper.

Once, I slammed my club into my golf bag with the force of driving an ax into a piece of wood. In my anger, I dented five of my new pinnacle iron shafts. I stood frozen in the middle of the fairway willing my rage to simmer. I was in big trouble and would have to pay to fix the clubs, but no one addressed my anger. "Just don't do it again," was all that was said.

Dad pushing my buttons didn't just happen with golf. I could be playing basketball or racquetball, whatever. The over-inflated tantrum, or the stuffing the steam internally, was put down to me needing to grow up and manage my competitive nature. That certainly was true. But no one ever reached out and asked what was going on, leaving me feeling utterly alone.

With each passing summer in high school, Dad and I played less golf together. I can come up with excuses for why—I was busy playing tournaments, working my summer job, playing with other kids—but the sad truth is that it just wasn't fun anymore.

14 // MY FIRST 9-HOLE TOURNAMENT

I watched the older kids tee off, my red and white carry bag tucked at my side. My clubs stood at attention, capped in pristine white headcovers stitched with the Twin Lakes Village emblem. As the big kids drifted into the golf course, I felt alone, a ten-year-old who had no idea what to do.

For over a year, I waited to join the Washington Junior Golf Association summer program. I thought I was ready to take on the golf world by storm. Finally, I was ten and eligible to play in the weekly 9-hole golf tournaments. Confident anticipation transformed into frantic butterflies in my belly as my first tournament loomed. Excited and anxious, I wasn't sure I would make it to my tee-time.

The morning of the tournament, I rode to Spokane with an older girl from my area: Jamie, a wise seventeen-year-old and one of the best female golfers in town. She paid attention to me and assured my parents she would look after me. I was proud to be in her company, but the butterflies still warred inside my little tummy throughout the forty-five-minute drive to Manito Country Club.

The older kids played eighteen holes for their tournament rounds, so they teed off before the eleven and younger age group. Jamie soon disappeared into the golf course with the rest. I stood there fidgeting. There were a couple hours before my tee time. I knew no one else, and I certainly was not brave enough to ask for help or strike up a conversation with someone new.

I retrieved my driver to practice, needing to keep myself occupied. I kept the headcover on the driver because it felt appropriate to wait until my first official swing in the tournament to remove it. I stood off to the side, squared up, and swung. The fuzzy, white protection sailed out in front of me and plopped into a wet patch of dirty grass, no longer clean and white. Who knows if anyone else saw the headcover flying in the air, but in my mind, a hundred pairs of eyes stared. I was caught in my false confidence, sure to be taken down by my pride. All I wanted was for someone to tell me everything was going to be okay.

I cannot remember a single shot I took during that tournament. I do remember the trophy, though. I won the eleven and under division with a sixty-three. The butterflies settled. A hundred pairs of eyes were on me, in a good way. People congratulated me. I couldn't stop smiling.

When I arrived home, trophy in hand, my dad's face beamed with pride. He scooped up the trophy and placed it on the family room bookshelf. I was hooked, not only on golf, but on my father's adoration of my newfound success.

My new goal: bring him more trophies to make him proud.

15 // DAD'S ATTENTION

Two towheaded trumpeters stood at attention before the TLV clubhouse, waiting for the Fourth of July celebration to commence. My left hand awkwardly jabbed my trumpet into my ribcage, while my other hand gripped the valves, pushing my right arm perpendicularly into my chest.

My father held his instrument with ease and poise. Dad looked comfortable and ready. I slouched, an awkward portrait of an eleven-year-old who was wearing a striped red and white polo shirt and bright red pants, which rose well above my waistline. My eyes bounced around, nervously taking in the faces and golf carts.

Everyone gathered around the flag, with Dad and me at the center of attention.

My father played trumpet most of his life. He found a way around the military draft by being accepted into the Air National Guard Band. His unit partied their way through the Vietnam War, playing for dignitaries and celebrations. After the military, he joined the local Coeur d'Alene Big Band and entertained at social events.

When it came to selecting what instrument I would learn to play in band class, I don't remember being asked what I wanted. I did what Dad did. I took up the trumpet.

Sometimes when I practiced, he would come down to the basement and grab my instrument. Suddenly Glenn Miller's "In the Mood" filled the house as if he was on stage with his band. I giggled and stared in awe at his ease with his horn.

Back on that Independence Day in 1983, there we stood, expert and novice on display to the community, to play "The Star-Spangled Banner." He played the main melody, of course. My novice lips blew the easier harmony notes. We also played together on a few cold Easter sunrise service mornings. I did not want to disappoint him, so I submitted to the duets and worked hard to improve. I loved and hated those mornings we played together.

16 // THE TRUNK

A curious child by nature, I loved to explore. Our basement contained a large playroom with carpet, a few pieces of furniture, a record player, and games. The egress windows filtered in some natural light, which played its own games against the finished walls. Two other rooms in the basement were not off limits, but they were not places to play.

On this afternoon, I decided to explore the storage room, although with trepidation. I turned the knob on the door, my quest to find treasure blocking the fear from my mind. Inside it smelled of musty concrete. Cobwebs and spiders lurked in the room's corners and among the boxes. The concrete floor cooled my socked feet. To the left, the extra freezer hummed as I scanned the narrow room beyond it.

Something caught my eye—a worn-out black trunk with faded brass edging. It was three feet long and two feet wide. Perhaps it had been there all along, and I only noticed it that day. I moved the few items off the lid and cracked the trunk open. It had to be my dad's.

Unfamiliar magazines, likely over a hundred of them, filled the container. *Playboy. Penthouse. Hustler.* There were also videotapes.

I wanted to flee, but curiosity held my feet in place. The unknown and forbidden pulled me in until a magazine rested in my hands. My eyes raced over images of naked bodies making my eleven-year-old body tingle.

Everything blurred around me. Time stood still until the pounding of my heart made me jump. I threw the magazine into the trunk, pulled the lid shut and anxiously threaded the straps tight. I ran out of the storage room, my confusion and shock pulling the door closed without turning out the light.

I ran upstairs, my mind swirling. *Why does Dad have that trunk. Does Mom know?* Without putting it into words, I knew I had to keep my dad's secret. A cold shiver surged through me as I considered for the first time that my dad was not safe.

It wasn't uncommon to be alone in the house for long periods while my parents were at work. Despite the initial repulsion, I started returning to the trunk. The magazines opened new feelings I had not known before.

I had no vocabulary for the yuck I felt. Something inside me knew this was bad, and it made me feel good too. I was not equipped to understand what was happening in my body.

One afternoon, I was caught. My mom found me alone in my bed. I pulled the covers over me to hide, but there was nowhere to go. Humiliation streamed down my face as I told her I found the magazines. Her tone was straightforward and emotionally flat, without anger. I cannot remember her words, but the I message I heard was this was bad, I was bad, and I needed to stop. End of discussion.

The trunk remained; it just shifted to a corner on the far side of the garage.

17 // A SIXTH-GRADE FIELD DAY

My friend and classmate Paige hovered a half-stride behind my left shoulder as I raced down the dirt track. The whoops and hollers of our classmates whipped by me. The wind blew my blonde bowl cut backwards. The finish line appeared ahead. I willed my legs to extend faster.

With puberty came an explosion of hormones, which crippled me on some days and pumped my muscles full of strength and coordination on others. As my athletic prowess surged, I realized I could use my gifts to my advantage.

Field day was the best day of the year in sixth grade. The sun and blue skies stood at attention above our little playground, giving a glow of glory to our athletic games. I waited eagerly for the events to begin, the warm spring air edging the green neckline on my classic white baseball T-shirt. The sleeves reached just past my elbows, and a green number 11 filled the front of my shirt. My short green shorts completed my outfit. I stretched my legs, bouncing up and down in anticipation. The movement shifted my white tube socks with a green stripe down my legs. This green and white athletic outfit would be my victory garb.

I wanted to win. I needed to win. I knew people were watching, classmates who I wanted to prove myself to. I strived so I could bask in the sweet indulgence of adoration. Not out of arrogance or a need for popularity. I simply wanted to fit in.

I competed with a fervor, intending to win every event. I jumped farther. I threw harder. I ran faster. The finish line approached. I ran faster than Paige, faster than everyone. The 100-yard dash was mine. I ran to win—for admiration, for acceptance.

18 // SWINGING THROUGH THE SUMMERS

Motorcycles, swimming, tennis, snowmobiling, and cross-country skiing enchanted my first decade of life. The summers of 1977 through 1989 were reserved for golf, and winters for basketball. Our warm golf season covered a few months and bookended with a month or two of colder weather.

Despite my tumultuous days of golf with my dad, I soon found a rhythm in the sport, devoting hours of my summers to the game. While other kids frolicked in the pool, escaped to—or lamented about—overnight camps, or sat bored at home, I practiced and played golf. On a rare afternoon, I made a brief appearance at our neighborhood pool, but even on those days golf was on the schedule too. I came to the pool from practicing in the morning or after picking the balls up on the practice range for my side job.

Sometimes when I left the pool, I headed out for a four-hole loop before dark. I routinely aimed my last drive off number nine tee directly at the side of our two-story house two-hundred yards down the right side of the fairway. Thankfully I never broke a window, but Mom was understandably not happy with me.

Shaking hands with Randy Henry on the practice range at Avondale GC was the most significant moment of my twelve years of life—and my budding golf career. Randy, a golf prodigy who suffered career-ending back injuries, designed a new way to fit and build custom golf clubs. Barely a year after brutalizing my Pinnacle iron shafts, I received my first of many sets of Henry-Griffitts golf clubs. Custom fit for me by lie angle, shaft flex, weight, and length.

Randy taught me how to swing with power and strength. Patient, encouraging, eccentric, and light-hearted was Randy. His care and kindness offered me stability. He believed in me before I (and many others) believed in me. Out of the hundreds of lessons I received from Randy, he consistently said, "Golf is a great game, you're going to do great, and it will lead you to something bigger in life." His words stayed close to my heart during the good and hard days. I am currently experiencing his wisdom in how my story continues to unfold.

In between my lessons with Randy, I played and practiced at Twin Lakes Village golf course. The practice putting green sidled up to the clubhouse. Practically shoved in a corner of the property, it was mostly flat. The limited space around the edges made practicing chipping boring. Putting and chipping were not my favorite skills to practice in the first place. Usually, I could be found on the driving range for hours, hitting ball after ball after ball.

19 // THE SUMMER SCHEDULE

Summer golf in the Pacific Northwest is where I forged my competitive skills.

I crisscrossed our neighboring state to the west with the Washington Junior Golf Association's (WJGA) program for eight summers. The WJGA welcomed residents of North Idaho to participate in all their events, and since Spokane, my district, was closer to home than driving to southern Idaho, I declared my allegiance to Washington Junior Golf. I also competed in regional tournaments run by the Pacific Northwest Golf Association, events where junior golfers from four different states gathered to compete. These events allowed me to set my sights on larger tournaments, like the PGA Junior Championship and the USGA Junior Championship.

The responsibility for all the expenses of competing as a junior golfer fell on my parents. The rules then prohibited any other support. There definitely were events that the lack of money and time prevented me from participating in. I'm pretty sure Mom took part-time work to help cover costs.

The summer I was thirteen, I didn't meet the age requirement to compete for the Washington State Girl's Junior America's Cup, a four-person team from each of the western states, British Columbia, and Mexico. I chose to travel south for a couple of Idaho Junior tournaments so I could earn a spot on the Idaho Junior America's Cup team at Shaughnessy G&CC in Vancouver, Canada. My allegiance quickly circled back to the Washington State team the following two years.

I participated in three USGA Junior Championships—*participated* being the deliberate word choice since any successful golf memories evade me, outside of qualifying for the championships. I put on a show of confidence as I traveled outside of the Pacific Northwest to play, but often I was scared to death. Usually, one of my parents traveled with me, but not always.

After completing the Girls Junior America's Cup tournament in Mexico City, Mexico, my Washington State teammates and I returned to Seattle, washed our clothes, repacked our suitcases, and caught a red-eye flight to Boston—all on the same day. After traveling overnight and across time zones, my fifteen-year-old self arrived at my host housing in South Hadley,

Massachusetts, feeling lost in space, completely disembodied.

I sat in the old front parlor room of my host housing, which enveloped me in a sea of white. I struggled to hold my body upright in a battle to not fall asleep. Alertness slipped away behind my bobbing eyelids. I longed for sleep, and for my mom.

The plan for the week was for Mom, who was flying in the next day, to stay in a local college dormitory while I stayed in host housing. My tough, independent exterior applauded the decision. When I climbed into bed that evening for sleep, I assured myself I would be just fine. I wanted to help save money by sticking with the arrangement, but tears burned and tumbled down my cheeks. I wanted to be with my mom.

I usually pushed through hard things and did what I perceived was expected of me. In this moment, feeling physically and emotionally depleted, I asked for what I wanted and needed. I broke down and asked if I could stay with my mom at the local college dormitory. After two nights in my host housing, I moved into the dorm room.

The following summer, heat and humidity welcomed the USGA Junior Championship to Golden Valley, Minnesota. I traveled without my parents this time for the whole week. Huge windows looked out from the clubhouse over a beautiful course. The view offered periodic respite. From there, I witnessed my first tornado flash before my eyes. The dark, blue-green sky squatted low over the course. Harsh rain and wind pummeled against the building. Intrigue pulled us toward the windows, despite warnings to stay away from them. And then it was over. The sky opened. The winds calmed.

Competitive golf can be the same way. One minute, you feel smacked and blown over. Then, a sudden momentum shift returns the calm. The game never stays static.

My third and last USGA Junior Championship took me across the country to Pine Needles, North Carolina—the home of Peggy Kirk Bell, professional golfer and golf instructor. Peggy was well known for her strong advocacy of women's golf. She welcomed us to the championship. All the participants gathered in the dark, musty theater room at Pine Needles Resort. The purpose of the meeting was informational, but Peggy spiced it up. She assumed the mic and conducted a competition right there on stage. I sunk low into my seat pretending to be invisible. To my dismay, she pointed right at me.

I stood on stage with a sea of faces staring back at me. A fellow competitor, Brandi, stood to my right. Peggy smiled and handed each of us an ancient-looking golf club and three Wiffle balls. Peggy then challenged us: How many of our Wiffle balls could we hit up into the balcony?

My legs disappeared from beneath me. *Who was I to be standing on this stage?* My heartbeat pounded. My hands sweated, and my face flushed red. We alternated shots. Brandi hit all three up into the balcony. I hit two over the edge and one line drive into the back wall. Peggy lightly teased me, not meaning any ill will.

The story my brain heard though was *you don't belong here* and *you're a failure*. Humiliated, I ran off the stage, head hung down.

20 // STERN AND LOVING HEARTS

The morning sun's glare blurred the silhouette of the fairway mower's driver. He moved down the ninth fairway toward the green. His ball cap hunched low on his forehead, making his squatty torso barely visible. I looked up from hitting balls with Randy and waved to the driver, PāPā, my grandfather.

PāPā's hard heart and demand for discipline didn't make for a warm relationship. Yet, when he retired from the Coast Guard, he and my grandmother, whom we called MāMā, moved to Coeur d'Alene, Idaho, to be near my mom and their grandkids.

While MāMā steadily worked an office job, PāPā took a multitude of jobs. He dabbled at being a mailman. He also drove a school bus, ruling his charges like the military man he was. When chaos broke out, all he needed to do was send his glare through the rearview mirror, and order was restored. But the kids loved him, a stark difference from how his own children felt when they were young. Decades after fully retiring, former students often approached him to say hello.

PāPā eventually softened with my sister and me. He wasn't a teddy bear of compassion and tenderness. He internalized his thoughts and emotions. Yet, whenever we visited, he welcomed a hug and kiss with a grin. He knew that as soon as I let go, I would dart into the kitchen to rummage through his sweets. His assortment never disappointed; there were vanilla sandwich cookies, wafers, Nutter Butters, or candy.

My grandparents' presence wove through my childhood. They showed up for sports and school activities. Holidays were shared, often Thanksgiving at their house and Christmas at ours. They babysat and, when I caused trouble, we waited for my dad's discipline, although one of their looks was often enough to stop my antics. Māmā's eyes could penetrate right through me. PāPā's glare could, too.

MāMā's grit ran deep from years as a Coast Guard wife. Her strength slipped out through a witty sarcastic remark, a roll of her eyes, or a straight-on reprimand. She later developed rheumatoid arthritis. Her smile deflected the pain in her twisted fingers and legs. She scorned the use of a cane. By the time we visited the World's Fair in Vancouver, she required a wheelchair.

We took full advantage of it, cutting to the front of lines and driving her around like an Indy race car. I slipped around sharp turns and popped the chair into wheelies. "Tracy Ann!" she bellowed from her belly. "Stop it!" Her stern eyes glared, but a grin peeked out from underneath.

My grandparents supported me and shared my interests. In addition to mowing fairways at Avondale Golf Course, PāPā also crafted golf clubs. After years as a USCG engine mechanic, he loved working with his hands. He tinkered with model airplanes and illegally recorded VHS films at home. His golf clubs were well-executed works of art. His cherry-colored woods, bright with polish, stood at attention like soldiers waiting for a ceremony to commence. He designed iron sets for friends, setting each shaft into the head with precision. I never did play his clubs, but I know, like him, they were something special.

21 // VROOM VROOM

After moving to Twin Lakes Village, my parents upgraded my motorcycle to a Yamaha 80 trials bike for my ninth or tenth birthday. (I can't recall which.) My dad rode a bigger trials bike, and I wanted one just like his. A trials bike was skinnier, built to balance and maneuver over obstacles. I thought it was so cool that my dad competed in trials races. But for someone my size, my new motorcycle contained a lot of power.

I wanted to test it immediately, even though the late October day was cold. Dad balanced the bike for me to climb on. My tiptoes barely touched the ground as I straddled the seat. I kickstarted it with a punch, full of confidence. The engine's power surprised me, and the response kicked in once again. I froze. The bike jolted forward, swerved left, right, and straight for a pine tree in our front yard. Fortunately, after the adrenaline subsided, all my body parts were accounted for and intact.

I rode that bike for a few years before I wanted, needed, a new one to keep up with Mike, my neighbor next door who was a few years older than me and raced motocross. Mom adamantly said no to racing, but I enjoyed trying to keep up with him.

So, I obtained a new Yamaha 125, my last childhood motorcycle. The Yamaha 125 had a white tank and a cool fender. This bike felt like a real adult bike. Mike's dad built us a small oval track with two jumps, one on each straightaway. We spent hours racing on the track and zooming around our small community.

Something shifted in me around age twelve. I no longer had someone to ride with. Our family stopped spending spring breaks in the dunes. So I set aside my love for motorcycles. I focused on golf and basketball during the summers. Also, riding a motorcycle didn't fit with what the other girls were doing. I wanted to fit in with them, even though I didn't know how to.

It was the end of an era.

My passion resurrected in my late thirties. I was a little nervous about getting back into bikes, but when I did, it felt like coming home.

I first bought a red sports bike and rode it for a while. Then I wanted something bigger and more comfortable. I found a Honda Shadow 750 with a white tank and fenders. This time around, the white tank and fenders unite my love for adventure and freedom with the goodness of my femininity.

22 // DRIBBLING TO SUCCESS

At the end of sixth grade, I was finally old enough for summer basketball camp, taught by the high school girls. I was giddy with enthusiasm. When I was much younger, the only organized sports I participated in were tee-ball and coed soccer. Now I gawked at the older girls casually dribbling, spinning basketballs from one hand to the other with gentle agility. I wanted those skills. I wanted to be the best one at camp.

Later that fall, I made the seventh-grade basketball team. I was ecstatic.

The games usually consisted of ten girls scrambling up and down the court. During our first game, a loose ball popped into my hands, and I charged toward a basket. No one ran after me as I executed a layup. The small crowd was loud, and I puffed with excitement. I slowed down at the sound of Coach Shaw's voice yelling at me from the sidelines. Humiliation flooded my face with heat as I realized I scored on the opposing team's basket.

My tube socks carried me through that first year of team basketball. I improved my skills tenfold, and our bumbling seventh grade team developed into a respectable eighth grade team. I absolutely loved our coach, Miss Linrud. She was positive and encouraged us on and off the court. I led the team alongside my next-door neighbor, Michelle.

Due to our abilities, the two of us were invited to try out for junior varsity the following year. The high school basketball world stirred with this news. If we were moving up to the JV team, where would that leave the freshman team? Our abandonment of the freshman team became a small controversy.

Michelle and I proudly made the JV team, but we were still nervous. We slinked our way into the gym for the first practice. My stomach twisted and turned with nausea. Wide-eyed and a bit naïve, we had no idea what we were walking into.

A booming voice caught our attention. The bouncing balls and squeak of the shoes ceased instantly. The varsity coach ordered us on the baseline, introduced his new JV coach, and then, for the next hour and a half, directed us through drills. I never worked out that hard. I visited the garbage can a couple times to puke. My body ached and could barely move that first week. Yet, I loved every minute of it.

A few years later, our coach was quoted talking about my early venture into high school sports, "When I first saw her play basketball as a freshman, she made her first two fifteen-foot jump shots. You could tell she was out of the ordinary."

23 // INTRO TO JESUS

My feet propelled me toward the small classroom at the end of the hall, but I couldn't feel my body. My sister and I each carried a little brown Bible, which felt clunky in the hands of a nine-year-old. I shyly walked into the room, like a foreigner crossing the border without identification. The other kids ran around the stale, brown room, laughing and cutting up. My sister and I clung to each other as the teacher's voice rose above the noise asking everyone to sit down.

For some reason, after we moved to TLV, my parents decided we needed to go to church. Up to that point, church had not been a major part of my childhood. Dad was raised in the Lutheran tradition by his grandparents. My mom had little spiritual upbringing. We started attending services at Shepherd of the Hills Lutheran Church in Rathdrum. My sister and I were told we would begin Sunday school classes.

I came in with little knowledge. The teacher expected us to follow her instructions at a quick pace, but she sounded like an adult in a *Peanuts* cartoon, warbly and incomprehensible. I had no idea that the Bible included multiple books or that those books contained chapters and verses. Luckily, one of my classmates leaned over and showed me where to turn the pages. As she helped me, my face flushed red, and my eyes focused on the stiff carpet where we sat.

During sixth and seventh grade, I attended confirmation classes to prepare for my public profession of faith, to reaffirm promises made during my baptism as an infant, to receive first communion, and to become an official member of the congregation. Honestly, since I was only twelve and thirteen years old during those years, I went through the motions to appease my parents. I memorized what I was taught so I could just finish the process.

We met over several long weekends. The church held retreats where we sat in hard plastic chairs, listened to boring lectures, slept on the floor, and ate lots of junk food. We spent other weekends at one of the kids' homes or a retreat center doing much of the same.

A few of the other kids and I usually found our way into trouble. Once, we snuck away during a break to drive a snowmobile across the frozen lake. It was a riot, until a big mean dog appeared and chased us down. It clamped its jaw around my Sorel boot and refused to let go. Our secret escape abruptly ended and soon, angry voices lectured us as we huddled together, staring at the frozen ground. My parents grounded me—a common occurrence—and I didn't care. It was no match for the thrill of the adventure.

Somehow, I made it to the altar railing at the front of the church. I knelt on a padded bench with my hands open and head bowed, secretly peeking to the left and right at my friends. Our pastor, decked in a white robe for the occasion, handed me a wafer and a little cup. I ate. I drank. I was a confirmed Lutheran.

Our family's church attendance dwindled after a couple years until we fell into the category of churchgoers who only appear on Christmas and Easter. When Dad and I played trumpet for the Easter services, I did it because Dad wanted us to do it. I hated being in front of everyone, holding my metal trumpet in the frigid, spring air.

Shepherd of the Hills Lutheran Church introduced me to Jesus, but the church and I pretty much left Him stuck in the Sunday school room. Whatever I learned about Him didn't change me.

Yet, God dropped His first spiritual seeds into my life. I didn't understand then that He loved me. Even if I had, it wouldn't have mattered because I believed that to be loved, I needed to perform a certain way. Why would God be any different?

Those lies devoured most of those spiritual seeds. The ones that survived fell deeper into the recesses of my heart. A time was coming, however, when the spiritual truths would get sprinkled with new water and grow into a path to new life and purpose. But not before years of pain.

24 // THE FORD ESCORT

Giddy with excitement, Debbie and I squinted through the glare of the sunlight bouncing off the white hatchback sitting in our driveway. A Ford Escort. We opened the car doors and jumped in, sliding onto the red interior. Debbie settled into the driver's seat, already licensed. I strapped into the passenger's seat.

"Go ahead. Take it for a drive," Dad motioned, cigarette in hand. And we did. Hundreds of drives, back and forth to school, into Coeur d'Alene, and around the backroads.

During my teen years, the state of Idaho allowed daytime driver's licenses to be issued to drivers as young as fourteen years old. The white Escort arrived in our family when I was thirteen. I had to patiently wait to *legally* drive it.

I already knew how to drive. My dad, always willing to color outside the lines, let me drive the family car on two-lane highways when I was eleven. He taught me how to drive a stick shift when I was twelve.

When I enrolled in driver's education, it seemed like a formality. At fourteen, it was unfathomable to me to not be a good driver. Why would I need to learn the actual rules of the road? Luckily, the course was mandatory. While I waited to finish my seemingly pointless driver's education course, I still wanted to drive the Ford Escort.

Bored and home alone one day, I stared at the white machine in the driveway. Temptation drove out common sense as I reasoned to myself, "I could just drive it around the village without any harm. People see me delivering the afternoon newspaper by other means of transportation. They wouldn't question me in a car."

I grabbed the keys and ran out the door. Adrenaline coursed through my veins as I turned the engine over. I shifted into reverse and eased out of the driveway. First gear jerked me forward and I was off. Instead of driving around the golf course as I planned, I headed for the entrance to Highway 41 and turned south.

I knew the way well, since it brought me to school in Rathdrum every day. My hands squeezed the wheel tight. My foot pressed hard on the accelerator. The car labored as it gained speed. My eyes focused on the road and exhilarated laughter filled in around me. The speedometer glided to 50 … 60 … 70 … 80 … 90 ….

A radar warning screamed out. It wasn't a cop, though. It was my own personal radar. I abruptly lifted my foot off the accelerator as reason seeped back into my consciousness. I pulled off the road, pointed the car north, and followed the speed limit until I safely parked the Escort back at home. I closed the garage door and walked into the house with my adventure tucked close to my heart, and a smile a mile wide.

25 // BOYFRIENDS

Upperclassmen rarely dated freshmen, but somehow a junior noticed me, a freshman. My heart thumped when he talked to me. He handled the heckling from his friends; the fact that we were in two different school buildings gave space for the teasing to cease. For a short period, he made me feel wanted and beautiful. Since I was only fourteen, our dates mostly consisted of him visiting our house under my parents' nominal supervision. Yet, I never felt like my parents "watched" over us.

He bravely asked me to prom, and I accepted. He looked so handsome in his tux, but I felt like a clown in my baby blue puff-sleeved gown. We danced, kissed, and made serious eyes at each other. My dreamy night overshadowed the awful prom dress.

Not long after prom, our parents allowed my sister and me to go with our boyfriends to our ski condo at Schweitzer Mountain Resort. Looking back, I can't imagine what they were thinking. But we jumped at the chance. We packed up the car and zipped out of the driveway, ready to be four teenagers alone for an overnight.

The sun shone high and bright in the sky when we arrived at the top of the mountain. A chill remained in the spring air. We dropped our belongings off at the condo, loaded up on picnic goodies, and explored the exposed ski runs. What a gorgeous day for a hike. Droplets of snow speckled the mountain. Lake Pend Oreille sprawled through the valley below. The sun's beams reflecting brilliant blue back to our eyes.

We returned to the condo exhausted. As the evening progressed, a tension gripped me. We all four ate, played games, and then…It did not occur to me until that moment what the rest of the evening might entail.

Suddenly, I realized what no parental supervision meant. I lost track of Debbie and her guy. My thoughts raced. *What was I thinking? What was he thinking?* We kissed and rolled around for a while. I was scared. I couldn't get any words out of my mouth. As clothing disappeared my body tightened in a way that said no to actual sex. Eventually we settled in for the night. Sleep abandoned me as I anxiously waited for the morning.

After a quiet breakfast, everyone loaded the car and drove home.

Not long after, he ended our relationship and I had my heart broken, the first of many times. (More than twenty years later, he contacted me and apologized for how he treated me. That meant a lot.)

A few other boyfriends came and went. They were typical high school relationships, and I use *relationships* loosely. We held hands in the hallways. Cheered each other on in our sports. Watched movies and made out on the couch. My parents rarely monitored our whereabouts.

A teenager's brain is only capable of being in the present reality. I never belonged to the "pretty girl" group so having a boy seek me out felt like a big deal. These adolescent relationships never had a chance, but it didn't feel like that in the moment of heartache after a breakup.

26 // STUCK UP

Musician.
Student of the month.
Student councilperson.
Team captain.
Basketball state champion.
Player of the year.
Honor Society member.
Valedictorian.
College golf scholarship recipient.
Golf prodigy.

My friends broke the news to me that some girls were calling me stuck up. Anger erupted. "Don't worry about them," they said, trying to calm me down. My eyes darted around the hallway, searching for the offenders. Embarrassed, I swallowed my hurt in silence and pretended to shrug it off. I would not show weakness. I hid the shame and sadness.

Maybe I did come off as arrogant sometimes. My junior high and high school résumés *were* impressive. Yet, my confidence was fragile.

I made sure no one knew, though. Once, a girl threatened my older sister, Debbie, over a boy. Debbie and I were complete opposites. Debbie was beautiful, petite, outgoing. Her voice sang out like an angel's. Despite being a year behind her, I was taller and stronger. We often checked in with one another. When I heard someone had threatened her, every muscle in my body contracted. I clenched my fists and, with a firm jaw, let the rumor mill work for me. I let everyone know that if anyone came after my sister, they would fight me first. Nothing further happened that day. But the message was sent—don't mess with me or my sister.

I carried that bravado into athletics as well. Best friend Michelle and I encouraged each other in sports. After joining the JV basketball team our freshman year, we quickly became a dynamic duo on the court. We played a few junior golf tournaments together, too. Michelle pushed me to sign up for volleyball camp the summer between our sophomore and junior years. I hardly knew the game since summer golf usually took priority when their season started in the fall. I usually cheered my friends on from the bleachers.

The first day of camp, I sauntered into the gym. Coach Claudia smiled and must have secretly taken pity on me. I pulled my knee pads up and listened to the instructions. We worked through some basic drills and did some cardio. Easy enough for me. Then, the game changer. Coach Claudia assigned one player to hit spikes toward a line of us on the opposite side of the court. Our objective was to dig the ball and roll out of it.

I observed the timing and grace of each player ahead of me. I thought, *I got this. I know how to roll.* I shuffled into position: a half squat, balancing on the balls of my feet, and my hands and arms stretched in front of me. The whistle screeched, and I eyed the ball. *Slam!* It came at me so fast. I jumped forward, completely missed the ball, and my attempt to roll out turned into a belly flop on the hard gym floor. Laughter filled the air.

My volleyball career began and ended in one day. I was okay with that.

Since grade school, I hated reading aloud or speaking in class. The first speech I presented was in Mr. Gordon's Sophomore Speech class. I acted cool on the outside, but inside, I was scared as hell. My stomach churned. My heart pounded. I wanted to vomit. A nervous laugh squeaked out of my throat as I scanned the room. The clock stared back at me. Mr. Gordon nodded, signaling me to start. I whispered, "You can do this. You can do this.:

Less than three minutes later, I fell into my seat, flushed and sweaty. I barely made it through. I acted like it was no big deal in front of my classmates. But it was a big deal. I was one of the smart kids. I participated in many activities. But there were certain academic hurdles I struggled with, and no one knew.

Our school did not have a cafeteria, so it was either bring your own lunch or converge on the concession stand for junk food. Prepackaged burritos, chips, candy, and cookies were the lot. Lunch was anywhere you found a place to sit. Our small group sprawled along the hall, a mix of athletes and nonathletes. Despite having a group of friends, I often felt like I didn't fit in. I could care less about the latest fashions or trends, but I still wanted to belong.

I was a model student, except for one class: Honors English, with Mr. Hanson (no relation!). I was on my way to a cumulative 4.0 GPA but with Mr. Hanson's class on my schedule, I could not work my way to perfection. Deciphering poems, literature comprehension, and writing papers was drudgery. I walked across his threshold every day, afraid. I fidgeted and felt anxious, especially when Mr. Hanson glared at me over his glasses. Yet, I had to take Honors English because all the other smart kids did. And I was one of them.

Even when classes came fairly easy for me, I pushed myself hard through high school. Near the end of 1989, my senior year, our principal called me into his office and informed me that I earned the valedictorian honor. I laughed. "Are you sure?" This was never on my radar, and surely there were other kids more worthy of the honor.

I did know that this was a very big deal. But the main thing that consumed my thoughts was the fact that I had to give a speech—the thing I hated most. As Chris, the kid I kicked in the mouth in fourth grade, and I walked down the aisle into the auditorium, "Pomp and Circumstance" played in the background. I felt a bond with Chris, and we always ended up in smiles and laughter together. When I stood to take the stage, he gave me a nudge and his eyes said, "You got this!"

27 // MAKING VARSITY

It was October in 1986, which meant basketball season had finally arrived. I had powered through my junior varsity season as a freshman, and I was ready—VARSITY READY—my sophomore season. Michelle was also pulled up to varsity by Coach, who had been promoted to the varsity head coach for the upcoming season. We had our sights on dominating and winning the state championship.

At 5 foot 7, my job was two-fold: point guard and shooting guard. If I wasn't chasing down a fast break, the rest of our plays were designed for getting me an outside shot or an easy layup. I accepted the task like a good soldier.

Along with our team being riddled with injuries, our sloppy play induced performance anxiety for all. My hopes of being district and state champs were crushed by our opponents, and I was not playing up to my potential. The season was a disappointment. We still had a lot to learn.

The next year, we were ready to forget our disastrous season from a year ago. Our two seniors and three juniors (including me) were the starting line-up. I felt the weight of expectations on my shoulders, and I hadn't even shot a basket yet.

Disaster again! One of our key seniors suffered an injury and our starting line-up was disrupted. Our bench of subs was not strong. I was back to point guard and shooting guard. With a losing record and a disappointing loss in the district tournament, our season was over.

28 // SCOOTER AND SHAGGY

With the force of my hand, I dribbled down the court for a breakaway layup. Over the din of the crowd, I heard one voice echo from the top bleacher, "Let's go, Scooter!" I hit my natural stride for a right-to-left leap toward the backboard. The ball rolled off my fingertips and softly banked into the basket. I made a quick U-turn and caught the eyes of the man who called me Scooter.

My collection of nicknames isn't deep. My close friends sometimes shorten my name to the typical Trace, Tray, or T. I was lucky enough to be greeted by Pat Bradley, LPGA Tour Hall of Fame member, with, "Hey, Pro."

Scooter was special, though.

Mike Shultz came into my life when his daughter, Jill, transferred as a sophomore to our high school. She and I played basketball together and became friends. Mike was a quiet, faithful attendee to all our games, always sitting in the back row of the bleachers at mid-court.

There was something special about Mike.

Our relationship mostly consisted of bantering, gently teasing in a way that always ended in laughter and smiles. I gravitated toward him when I wasn't on the court. He was one of the few men in my life who offered me a safe, unconditional presence. He coined my nickname during the first winter he watched me play basketball. He said Scooter fit me perfectly because I scooted the ball up and down the court with energy and intensity.

I held the nickname close to my heart. I still do. I only allow a few people to call me Scooter, in memory of the man who gave it to me. It's not a nickname suited for the professional golf world, but it fit the blue-eyed, blonde high school basketball player who scooted up and down the court like she owned it. The echoes of his voice yelling, "Scooter!" from the stands spurred me on.

One winter, I evened the playing field and gave Mike his own nickname. He had decided to grow his beard out that season instead of his clean-shaven look. As the facial hair grew thicker and thicker, I stumbled onto the nickname. I abandoned calling him Mike and started to address him as Shaggy. I was the only one he allowed to call him that.

Only a few years later, Shaggy was ushered unexpectedly into heaven at the way too early age of forty-four. A heart attack. When I think of him, I can still see him, elbows on his knees, leaning forward as he cheered us on. There's a nook in my heart, at the top of the bleachers, where Shaggy and Scooter still banter.

29 // "I JUST CAN'T"

"What do you mean, you're quitting band?" Miss Hubble, my band director, fumed.

The year before she gave me a solo to perform at our stage band spring concert. She hoped to build my confidence. I struggled to memorize the notes, even though it was only four measures long. During the concert, I tensed up. My muscles tightened so much that I could barely press the valves down. I slurred my way through the notes well enough to elicit claps from the bleachers in front of us. I slinked back to my seat, glad it was over.

"I don't have time for practice with golf and basketball," I squeaked out.

Practicing my trumpet had become tedious and a burden. Pep band. Stage band. Concert band. I didn't want to play anymore.

Basketball was different. My circuits fired when I felt a ball in my hands with the game on the line. I wanted to dedicate myself to sports and take new classes. "I have other things I want to do."

Miss Hubble's eyes bulged in her red face. Speechless for a moment, she tried switching tactics. She changed her voice and softly pleaded, "You're going to be first chair. I need you, Tracy."

Our best trumpeter, Mark, was not playing next year. I was next in line.

"I can't, I'm sorry. My dad will be disappointed, too. But I just can't." I walked away, guilt shadowing me.

With band out of the way, I could explore more classes like Spanish and computing. I could add advanced PE as a fun class. In the second semester, I could accept the invitation to be a teacher's aide for Coach. What better way to finish my senior year?

30 // HIGH-PRESSURE GOLF

"Did you just love high school golf?" a new acquaintance asked.

"Actually, no, I didn't. I hated high school golf." The words flew out of my mouth.

I quickly tried to rephrase. "It's not that I hated high school golf, but it wasn't the most fun. We played in the spring when it's cold and wet. I had to play on the boys' team because we didn't have any other girls interested except when I talked my best friend Michelle into playing our senior year."

A surprised and confused face stared back at me.

The truth is I always felt pressure to outperform the boys on my team in high school league play. I struggled to enjoy the season and often fell short of my potential.

Thankfully, high school golf in Idaho was not a make-or-break experience for my future career. The memories I have are not about the results but about the playing experience. While my teammates accepted me and generally liked me being on the team, boys from other schools did not like getting beat by a girl.

We practiced at my home course, my 9-hole public course at TLV where I lived on the 9th hole. I think this helped me feel more comfortable at practice. They were in my territory. And I loved the convenience too.

I had already felt the expectations to be the best basketball player on our school team. But the pressure escalated tenfold as I became known as the local golf prodigy.

By the time I reached high school, I was already setting records in the Pacific Northwest Region. I had won the Washington State tournament at age fourteen and beat all the older girls. I felt like people expected me to conquer the high school golf program. The reality was yes and no.

On Saturday mornings, we met in the school parking lot. I would pull in, still a bit sleepy anticipating the long day ahead. Our 18-hole matches were played at different courses in our district. We all piled into the team station wagon. Being the only girl, Coach kept an eye on me and always had me sit next to him in the front seat. I felt special and awkward in that middle seat.

On the way to the match, we'd stop for orange juice and donuts. I usually went for a maple bar and a plain glazed. None of us had a clue about nutrition and thought it was a breakfast of champions. Knowing what I know now, it certainly reveals one significant reason why I never played as well during those Saturday rounds. The sugar crash melted me into a sluggish performance.

Springtime in North Idaho was unpredictable. We had to play in rain, cold, and sometimes snow. Misery with a capital M. As a girl on the boys' team, I had to play from the same set of tee markers as they did. For the most part, that didn't bother me. What sucked was that when our team played in state and I still shot lower than all the other girls who played the forward tees, I was not given the win. I couldn't compete as an individual in the girls' state tournament because the rules stated all girls had to compete from the same set of tee markers.

During my senior year, I had to decide prior to our district tournament to either play as a girl or as a boy. One or the other, period. If I chose to play for the girls' state title, I felt I would be letting my team down. If I chose to play on the boys' team, I might not make it to state at all.

In the end, I chose to play for the individual girl's title. The team failed to make it to state, but I qualified with ease for the state championship to be played in Jerome, Idaho. I was super excited because Michelle qualified too.

Michelle and I, plus Coach and our parents, drove eight and half hours to Jerome Country Club for our one-day competition. This would be my first official State B championship. The course played shorter than I was used to because I now played from the forward tees. My long drives enabled me to hit all the par-five holes in two.

I found my groove and really hit the ball well. After going out in 38 strokes on the front nine, I blitzed the back nine with a 35. I played focused all day and my 73 was 10-strokes ahead of the next competitor. A satisfying end to my high-school golf career, State B Girls golf champion.

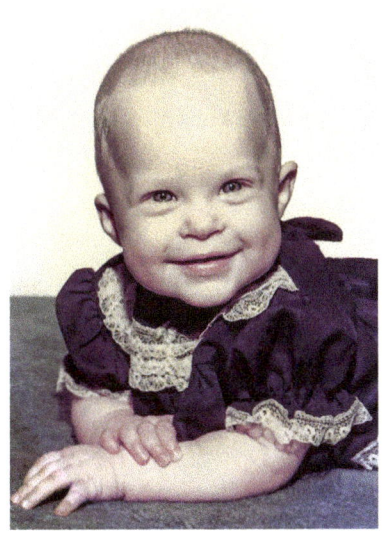

Me at 7 months old as Tracie Ann Hanson. Three years later, Mom would legally change my name to Tracy.

Perched with Dad on HONDA in May 1973. One and a half and ready to fly like the wind.

A giant grin at my new Tonka truck in 1975, the best Christmas Day ever.

At 4 years old riding my mono-bike in the woods on Royal Highlands in Post Falls, Idaho.

Mom, Dad, Debbie, and me (bottom left; age 6) in my favorite Royal Highlands home overlooking the prairie.

My first tournament, and my first trophy, at 10. Manito Country Club, Spokane, Wash.

In 1977, Field Day, the best day in sixth grade. I'm the green 11 and I had to win the 100-yard dash. And I did.

Around age 12. I was blessed with a natural swing from the beginning. Soon after, I would meet Randy Henry, my longtime swing coach.

PART TWO:
THE DURING

31 // SPECIAL TREATMENT

When Coach invited me to weight train with the football team, I was thrilled. The players questioned why I, the only girl, was there, but I didn't care. I didn't have any equipment at home, I wanted to learn how to prepare better for my senior year basketball season, and besides, Coach had invited me.

I loved pushing my body to its limits. With every squat, deadlift, bicep curl, and box jump, I could feel myself getting stronger. When I stood terrified in front of the plyometric boxes—how could anyone jump up three feet onto this giant square without cracking their skull open—Coach was right beside me. "You can do it," he said encouragingly. "Jump."

I bent down, swung my arms backward, and pushed from my feet with all my might to propel my body upward. The balls of my feet landed square on the box and for a split second I froze. Had I really just done that? I smiled excitedly and watched Coach break into a huge grin, nodding. I knew I had made him proud.

At the first football game of the fall, Coach handed me a clipboard. I was one of three sideline statisticians for our high school team, and he emphasized that I needed to stay close to him. As far as I know, I was the only one he said that to.

Our Lakeland High School football team was a powerhouse my senior year. I walked the sidelines as the guys crushed every opponent on their way to the state championship game. We statisticians couldn't ride on the team bus to Idaho State University for the game, so we piled into a van with Coach's wife, dad, and mom. Thankfully, we were able to catch some sleep on the eight and half hour drive to southern Idaho.

Grabbing our bags, we shuffled into the dormitory where we were assigned to stay the night before game day. Coach and his wife were ahead of me as we walked down the hallway to our respective rooms. I turned my door handle and looked up just in time to catch Coach turn around and lock eyes with me. Shivers shot through my body. I felt unnerved and quickly shut the door of my room behind me and stood there, dazed.

What just happened? Why is my heart racing? Confusion settled around me like a dense fog. The unexpected and unwelcome physical feelings scared me. To make them stop, I distracted myself by getting settled into my room. *I must be overreacting. It was nothing,* I told myself.

The next day, the team moved up and down the field like a well-oiled machine. The state championship victory closed out the fall sports and everyone's attention shifted to the basketball season.

32 // "IT'S COACH TO YOU"

I shouted his last name from across the basketball court.

Spinning around with fire in his eyes, he spewed, "It's *Coach* to you."

It was obvious "Coach" was in a bad mood today. Practice wasn't going so well, and we were paying the price. I was a senior now and after four years of leadership under this man, I was used to his temper tantrums. I learned to lean into his intensity and refuse to break, for my own resolve and for the sake of the rest of the team.

Coming off a disappointing junior season, the starting seniors—Daisy, Heather, Michelle, and me—were hungry. All of them but me were still feeling the sting of an agonizing finish in their volleyball state run. But we were the school's best girl athletes and had played together for two years. Our team had all the goods to win the A-2 Class state championship: four experienced seniors plus a junior as the starting five supported by a deep bench.

Before I could suck in enough air, Coach's whistle blew again.

"Everyone on the line, down and back," he shouted. I knew his foul disposition would pass. I was familiar with Coach's patterns, maybe too familiar. One of us would make a great shot or an exemplary play and he would simmer down until the next perceived failed effort. In the meantime, he didn't make it easy on us. In an act of silent rebellion, I contorted my face into a piercing glare every time he looked in my direction, which was more often than not.

We were on track and in a solid position with only a few games before Christmas break. Our next game was against Post Falls High School—our conference and across-the-prairie rivals.

The air in the Post Falls High School gym was intense as the scoreboard lead jumped back and forth. Sprinting down the court on a fast break, I stuttered my stride for a layup on the right side of the basket. As my body was still moving upward, a Post Falls player collided with my legs. I saw the ball bounce off the basket, but something was seriously wrong.

In a split-second reaction, both my hands reached backward as gravity pulled me down and I hit the floor—hard. Hearing the whistle blow for the foul, I sprang to my feet to walk off the hit and catch my breath. As I stumbled toward the free-throw line, a wave of pain so great washed over me that I wasn't sure I could keep standing let alone make another shot. My left thumb instantly swelled to twice its normal size and I couldn't move it. I swallowed my tears and walked a few circles around the free throw line.

I ran over to the sideline to show Coach, but he pushed me back on the court and demanded that I go shoot my two free throws. It was a close game, and we needed the points. The ref threw me the ball and I winced. I bounced the ball once, then twice, but I couldn't get my left hand into position to shoot. I looked over at Coach, pleading with every ounce of my aching body to take me out. Finally, the whistle blew for an injury time out and my night was over. I felt like a failure.

After a trip to the emergency room the next day, my fears were confirmed. My left thumb was broken, and I would be benched the last two games before Christmas break. Furious, I watched from the bench as our team lost both games.

After a few days off for Christmas, I joined my team at the gym. The doctor had said no practice for two weeks but that didn't mean I couldn't work on my dribbling or my right-hand shooting technique. I just needed to find a way to get back on the court.

Once I was back in school, I made sure I continued icing my thumb several times a day. It was inconvenient, but Coach was willing to help. He pulled me out of government class early and had an ice bucket waiting for me in his classroom.

33 // HOME VISITS

Coach greeted me with a familiar smile at the front door of his small home and motioned for me to step inside. I hadn't known what to make of his invitation to dinner. None of my teammates had received an invite. Just me. His wife, who turned and smiled when I arrived, was busy cooking in the kitchen. The dining room table was to the left of the entryway and their living room was off to the right. I stood awkwardly, unsure of what to do next.

Was there a protocol for this situation? Girls' varsity basketball coach invites team captain (and only one of the team captains) over for dinner? My parents knew where I was going but didn't ask details, as was typical. And I certainly didn't tell my teammates or other friends.

Coach motioned for me to sit at the table. I accepted a glass of water and waited. We ate a dinner of tomato soup and grilled cheese sandwiches while I followed the conversation to the best of my ability, answering their questions. It felt strange and special at the same time. Was this a normal thing coaches did? Shortly after we finished eating, I said my goodbyes, jumped into my Volkswagen Rabbit, and focused on driving the five miles home.

34 // WE WON

Everything we had been working toward for the last four years was in front of us. We made it to the A2 State Championship game and it was my last chance as a senior. Coach challenged me before the game, "They're going to shut Daisy off. You're going to have to shoot the ball a little bit. You're just going to have to play. I'm putting all this pressure on you. Do you like all that pressure?"

Without missing a beat, I said, "Yes, I do."

We shuffled into the locker room at the half, Coach's hot anger following us. We had struggled and played nervous basketball through the first two quarters and left the court trailing 28–27. Once back on the court I picked up the pace, closing our gap but I couldn't take the lead. Kuna High School's defensive pressure had rattled us.

Michelle found her zone and was playing one of her best games of the year. She hit four long-range buckets at key moments. In the third quarter, her final bucket, along with four determined points by Daisy, gave us the lead, 40–32. We had momentum. Kuna couldn't pinch Daisy off the whole game. She fought for her space in the key, ultimately claiming 17 points. Heather's presence on the court grounded the team. In the span of one minute in the third quarter, we forced four Kuna turnovers.

Michelle jumped into action at the basket. Then everything spun into slow motion. I watched Michelle go down hard on the floor, writhing in pain. The gym went silent as the whistle echoed.

Our assistant coach jumped off the bench and ran to her. My heart sank watching Michelle get carried off the court. We just lost one of our key players and my go-to teammate. Was the state championship slipping through our fingers?

When the buzzer blared at the end of the third quarter, our lead had slipped to only two points.

I huddled the team together and fiercely said, "We got this. We need to win this game for Michelle." We blitzed out of that huddle and took Kuna by the throat. When Michelle reappeared on crutches and sporting a bandage on her leg in the fourth quarter, we never looked back.

We claimed our Idaho A2 Girl's State Championship victory. Everyone contributed, including the bench players. I dug deep and played my best game of the tournament finishing with twenty-four points, five steals, and four assists—and the tournament MVP honor.

I climbed the ladder soaking in the moment. Shaking, I clipped the first piece of net and raised it high in my left hand. My tear-stained cheeks broadened into a huge smile as I took in the cheers. When my feet hit the floor, I turned to Michelle.

"Your turn. I got you," I said. Michelle hopped up the ladder on her good leg.

After the cutting of the net and the trophy presentation, the quiet of the locker room welcomed us. Hugs and tears and laughter filled the space. The weight of our last time together as a team settled on us, meshing with the excitement of victory. Coach sat on a bench in front of the lockers holding the trophy for a long time.

The excitement was still palpable as we took our seats the next day for the bus ride home. The previous night was the culmination of four years of hard work. Our goal all along had been to win the Idaho state basketball championship and we did it.

I grabbed the third seat back on the right and settled in for the long ride back to North Idaho. Coach and his wife were in their usual front left seat. A couple hours into the drive, Coach started working his way around the bus. He plopped himself down in my seat and we chatted about the tournament and our goals. "We did it," he whispered.

He wasn't sitting close, but I felt something brush against my left pinky. Suddenly, a zing shot through my body. I froze. Before I could gain my composure, Coach was gone.

35 // COLLEGE VISITS

I was under pressure to earn a college golf scholarship. Area basketball coaches were disappointed when I made my intentions known that I would only pursue golf.

Coach helped me put together a VHS tape highlight reel and playing resume during my junior year. The summer before my senior year I sent tapes to schools with big golf programs. But I felt so uncertain. Who was I to think I could compete with the nation's best?

I plotted my way through the summer tournaments. My best finish was winning the PGA Junior National Sectional Qualifying tournament, earning a spot in the PGA National Junior Championship to be played in St. Louis, Mo. I played mediocre at best, but I did meet several college coaches throughout the summer.

One of the schools on my wish list was UCLA, with one of the best women's golf programs in the country. Randy, my swing instructor, personally knew the women's golf coach, opening the opportunity to send my packet to her. I didn't hear back for a long time.

My stomach swirled when the UCLA coach finally called and said she'd like me to come for a campus visit. I almost dropped the phone in shock. "Yes, I would love to come visit," I squeaked out.

When my plane landed, she was there to greet me. It felt surreal. We walked outside into the warm California sunshine. But within a matter of minutes, it all changed. The car weaved in and out of traffic toward campus. The intensity of Los Angeles overwhelmed me. I knew instantly I could not go to school at UCLA. I wanted to turn the car around and get right back on a plane.

As a NCAA Division I recruit, I was allowed to take five all-expense-paid college visits. Another school on my list was the University of Kansas. Two things attracted me to Lawrence, Kansas. One, my friend Shelly was on the golf team. And two, I had an unrealistic belief that I could play both basketball and golf there. The Kansas coach entertained my naiveté as we walked into the basketball arena. In my heart, I already knew I had to make my commitment solely to golf. And Kansas was not the place I was going to blossom.

So, I set out for the desert. I visited the University of New Mexico, New Mexico State, and University of Arizona. The University of Arizona would have been a winner, except the coach could only offer me a partial scholarship. Our family finances required a full scholarship for me to go out of state and I had to turn that offer down. The two New Mexico schools felt far from home, but New Mexico State made it into my top two choices because I liked the positivity of the coach.

After I had taken my five allotted NCAA visits, there was one more school I wanted to check out. A friend I'd played junior golf with was already signed to play at San Jose State University. I was told early on there were no available scholarships there, so I had taken it off my list. Still, something about being at a school where I knew someone on the team felt good.

By now it was February and the pressure to decide on a school was mounting. Then, out of the blue, I got the call that a scholarship at San Jose State had become available.

I knew nothing about San Jose—both the school and the city—when I told my parents I wanted to look at the school. I felt stuck and unsure. If I was going to visit, we would have to pay for the trip. But Mom was always up for a road trip. I loved that about her.

"Mom, what do you think?" I asked. Our plan quickly came together. Mom, me, and MāMā, my grandmother, would drive to San Jose over spring break. This wasn't the first time the three of us took on California. When I was eleven, we had traveled to San Diego for my first World Junior Optimist tournament.

This time, the sun had already set as we merged onto Interstate 680 West. I sat upright in the back seat. As we crested a hill, the expanse of the southern end of the Bay Area swallowed the horizon. Lights twinkled everywhere. "Oh my gosh, I don't know if I can go to school here," I said.

Mom helped calm my nerves. We got to downtown San Jose and drove around in circles looking for our Holiday Inn. All of us were punchy with laughter. Finally, we arrived and trucked our bags into our home for the next three nights.

I met the coach, the team, and the staff in the athletic department first thing the next morning. The school campus barely covered a square mile in the middle of downtown San Jose, and we were in an old, two-story building nestled on the southside of campus. This did not feel like a "golf" school. But somehow, the program had won the national championship the year before and was on target for a repeat.

I liked everyone I met and had a good feeling, but when I drove away from the fast-paced, densely populated Bay Area, I was not convinced this was the place for me.

Once we got home, I had about a month to make a final decision before the April national signing day. The decision felt heavy and big. Where did I want to spend the next four years of my life? And where would I fit in—New Mexico State or San Jose State?

On a late afternoon, I pictured two coaches counting minutes as they waited for a call. With crossed arms as I leaned against the pass-through between our kitchen and living room, ignoring the conversation in the room, I startled myself.

I raised my chin and blurted, "I'm going to San Jose State."

36 // DINNER ALONE

I realized immediately that something was different. I had walked through the front door of Coach's home before, but this time I scanned the rooms and realized we were the only two in the house.

"Are we alone?" I asked, knowing the answer but hoping I was wrong.

Coach glanced at me over his shoulder, nodded, and returned to stirring a pot on the stove. My thoughts were swirling, and I almost didn't hear him say, "I'm making venison. Have you ever tried it?"

I managed to squeak out a quiet, "No."

I was a young naive seventeen-year-old but this sure didn't seem right. What was I doing there all alone? I felt unsettled. Still, there was a hesitant pull to stay and join Coach for a venison dinner. He'd gone through all the trouble of cooking it, after all.

The minutes ticked by slowly as I choked down the gamey meat. My stomach twisted itself into knots, which made eating quite laborious. We made small talk and otherwise sat together at the table awkwardly. I presented myself as cool, collected, and engaged, a stark contrast to what was happening inside my body.

The thoughts, "Leave. Run out the door. Go. Now is your chance," were so deafening that I was shocked that Coach couldn't actually hear them. My brain was doing its absolute best to warn me, to protect me, but my body wouldn't budge. I couldn't move.

Coach got up from the table and moved into the living room. He motioned for me to follow. I sat rigid. The room was cast with shadows as the sun set in the early spring evening. Coach started talking.

I wasn't listening until I heard him say, "The only thing I want is to see you undressed."

I caught his eyes for a split second and immediately looked down at the floor. I didn't dare lift my gaze again that night.

"That's all you want me to do?" I asked. Would that be enough for him? I felt as if I was being pulled into a deep, black hole.

I slowly undressed. I could feel him looking at me, inspecting me from top to bottom. I shivered as heat radiated through my body. I was mortified, scared, exposed. The only possible survival plan I could conjure up at the moment was to pretend to be invisible. I stared at the floor, willing it to be over.

"You're beautiful and lovely," Coach said. "Thank you for letting me see."

Foggy and lightheaded, I hastily put my clothes back on, ran out the front door, and jumped in my car. My heart was in my throat and I couldn't catch my breath. The sweat from my palms made it difficult to insert my key into the ignition.

Drive. Go. Get out of here, Tracy.

The car finally started, and I pulled out of Coach's driveway.

The familiar sound of my blinker and the hum of the engine were comforting. It was the first time anything had felt the least bit comfortable all night.

The more distance I put between Coach's house and me, the more confused and ashamed I felt. What would everyone think of me now, Tracy Hanson, the star athlete? Would anyone believe me? Maybe I deserved it? Had I brought this on myself? What had I done?

37 // IT'S OKAY

"Mom, I'm going up to Sandpoint to play Hidden Lakes Golf Course with Coach after school." I disappeared out the door before waiting for her response.

In the several days since the night we had dinner alone, Coach had smoothed over my unease. He acted like everything was normal, even when he passed me notes before the first-class bell. His eyes were playful and scary at the same time. Ambivalence started to consume me. I didn't want his special attention anymore, and I was stuck in a magnetic pull toward him.

The afternoon was cool, still being early spring, but at least the sun was out. As a young senior, energy pulsed through my body and the school days were a slow crawl. When the last bell rang, I sprang out of class to my locker, grabbed the books needed for later, and ran out to my car. I exchanged my backpack for my golf clubs. I walked around the school building to the staff parking area where Coach was waiting by his car with the trunk open. I threw my clubs in and jumped in the passenger seat. A combination of unease and glee waffled through me as I climbed into the front passenger's seat.

The drive to Sandpoint was just under an hour. Awkward conversation volleyed back and forth as I watched the lakes and pine-filled mountains pass by. We passed familiar stores on Main Street, ones my family would frequent during winter ski season, and then the car turned to head up the mountain to Schweitzer Mountain Resort where my parents kept a ski condo. It was the same condo my sister and I, and our boyfriends, had spent the night at a couple years before.

My heartbeat pounded against my chest wall. I focused on the sunlight reflecting off the remnants of snow still packed in the shadows of the mountain road and labored to breathe. Twenty minutes later, the main parking area filled the horizon and I pointed to the left, directing him to the condo's parking spot.

We climbed the narrow stairway. With shaking hands, I inserted the key into the door of the condo. He sensed my panic and with his hand on my shoulder said, "It's going to be okay." I gave him a quick tour of the quaint two-bedroom unit and pointed out the window to the slopes I loved. I started skiing when I was ten and became quite good. The family had season passes and we would come up on weekends as frequently as possible.

He led me up to the top bunk in the bunkroom, saying something about a better view. The afternoon sun warmed and brightened the room. I laid there unsure what was going to happen next.

At first just his eyes traveled up and down my body. I tightened. Then he leaned in from my right and kissed me. I felt his hand move over my chest and thighs. It wasn't the first time I had been touched by a boy, but I was petrified. He said, "It's okay. Try to relax."

When he worked his way under my clothing, both desire and dread welled up from my insides. He took my hand and showed me what he wanted me to do.

The room darkened as the sun disappeared behind the mountaintop. With a glance at his watch, he sat up and said, "We'll stop and get a pizza on the way back."

I can't recall anything of the drive back to Rathdrum. The light overlooking the school parking lot didn't lighten the inner darkness I felt when I got out of his car. I numbly placed my clubs in my trunk and watched his taillights disappear with leftover pizza for his wife.

38 // MY CADDY

It had been three months since I played my last high school basketball game. Now, under Coach's eye, I had the job of guarding the best player on the court in the Idaho Girls All-Stars game. I couldn't hang with this Stanford University-bound guard, but a still-hungry desire to play college basketball fueled a drive to drop in 16 points of my own. That's how I officially ended my basketball career. A 10-foot jumper at the buzzer by the West team ended the back and forth, defeating my East team by one.

Before my sweat could dry, I knew golf was my destiny.

The next day was the start of it. After coaching the All-Star game, which was held at Capital High School in Boise, Coach volunteered to stay behind and be my caddy for a golf tournament only six miles away. Time to segue to the John Dropping Junior Memorial Championship. Last year I placed third. With my current record, my caddy and I both felt certain I could win it this year.

Coach had arranged to stay with his grandparents during the tournament, and I was invited to stay there too. After my parents dropped me off the next day after the basketball game, they started the seven-hour drive back to Northern Idaho. Coach's wife flew back to Spokane, just across the North Idaho state line.

The old house had lots of little rooms and squeaky wooden floors. I dropped my bags in one of the upstairs guest rooms. Coach was in another room across the small hall. The grandparents' bedroom was tucked away in a corner on the main level below.

Later that afternoon, as Coach and I walked around Hillcrest Country Club for my practice round, the foothills of the Sawtooth Mountains filled the horizon. The green fairways were a stark contrast to the brown hues of the hillsides. I felt light and joyful, and ready to play the tournament the next two days.

After a hearty dinner and light conversation with Coach's grandparents, I was tired and excused myself upstairs. I laid out my golf clothes, brushed my teeth, and climbed into bed. I wanted to fall asleep, but my body remained tense and anxious. I waited in the darkness of my room.

The encounters back home had been increasing, and I felt caught in a current out of my control. I didn't want him to come to my room, but I knew he would.

Unsure of how much time had passed, I felt Coach creep into the room and crawl under the covers next to me. I was so nervous that one of his grandparents was going to make their way upstairs to inquire if everything was okay. Noise carries well in old houses. He slipped away to his room an hour or so later.

After breakfast, we headed to the course for the first round of the tournament. I was excited and nervous. Coach assured me I was ready and that he was there to support me.

The fifty-four-hole tournament was to be played over two days: eighteen holes the first day and thirty-six holes the second day. I shot a seventy-four my first round and left the course with an eight-shot lead. I made some mistakes along the way but held it together.

My second night at Coach's grandparents felt like déjà vu. Dinner. Conversation. Tournament prep. Climb into bed. A visitor.

Day two was going to be a long one. Round two started at first light. I ended with another seventy-four and a commanding seventeen-stroke lead on my closest competitor. I was even the low score in the clubhouse, boys included. I was determined not to let down.

In the final round, I was playing for as many birdies as I could, not for par, which meant opening the door to bogeys. I made both, finishing with a seventy-five and a nineteen-stroke victory.

I stood next to Coach after the awards ceremony, proudly holding my trophy in front of us for pictures. I don't remember what words we exchanged, but I do know Coach's smile said he was proud of me. We left for the airport directly from the course to catch our flight back to Spokane and home.

The summer was going to be full of tournaments, and challenges. I wasn't eighteen yet, so I was still eligible to play in all the junior events I wanted to, but I had to report to San Jose State University in late August. It was time to forego the Washington State Junior Championship and pass the baton to the younger girls. My sole focus was on three national events: the Women's Western Junior Golf Championship, the USGA Junior Girls Championship, and the PGA Junior Championship.

"I'm not sure she amazes me anymore. She used to, but not now," Coach told the press after I cruised to a nineteen-shot victory at the United States Golf Association Junior qualifier in Tacoma, Washington. Thirty-six holes in one day tests not only the player, but also the caddy.

I liked having a caddy. I conserved more energy for my round and this qualifier was proof of that. I not only put my two best rounds together—seventy and seventy-one—I also set a new women's competitive course record at Spanaway Golf Course and earned my ticket to the USGA Junior Championship in Pine Needles, North Carolina, to be played in late July.

At the first tee of the Women's Western Junior Golf Championship match, I shook the hand of a player named Robin. We learned that we were going to be teammates at SJSU. But today, we were competitors. She would become the last player standing between me and the Championship trophy. I already defeated two girls, two nationally ranked amateurs, in my first two matches.

Coach had driven me the five hours across Washington State to Millcreek CC for the tournament and easily fell into his caddy role. By now, being alone together in the car felt normal and conversation was light and casual. My dad came for the competition days, and my host family was in the gallery too.

After losing the first hole, I was mad. My nerves strangled my muscles as I stomped to the second tee. Coach told me to relax and play my game. Over the next ten holes Robin and I jostled the lead back and forth, and left a hole tied four different times. With a two-up lead and birdie on the fourteenth, my concentration slipped again, and I lost hole fifteen with a three putt. With Coach's encouragement, I refocused and parred the next two holes to win the match one up.

As I talked with Robin afterward on the green, I noticed Coach walking over to my bag. My dad came up and extended him a congratulatory handshake. My dad's blind naiveté made my stomach twist. *How can Dad be so oblivious to what's going on?*

The three of us waited together for the trophy ceremony. A reporter asked what I thought about my win: "It means I've finally put myself on a national level, but it hasn't sunk in yet."

39 // ALMOST

My heart was racing.

The house was quiet except for the sound of my feet brushing the carpet as I paced back and forth. Every few seconds I peeked out my upstairs bedroom window looking for his silver S10 truck. I undressed and waited. I sat on the edge of my bed just to stand back up a second later to start pacing again.

The secret encounters were more than I could count by now, but I was still so nervous. When I heard a car door slam, I jumped. I didn't see his truck in the driveway.

Then I heard my dad's voice yell out, "Anyone home?"

I catapulted to my feet, grabbed my clothes from the floor, threw them back on, and yelled, "Hi Dad! I'm up in my room."

I ran down to the kitchen. "What are you doing at home?" I asked, trying (and failing) to act naturally.

He mumbled something that I didn't catch. It was hard to hear over the sound of my heart pounding in my ears. I wasn't really listening anyway.

"What are you doing?" he asked.

"Getting ready to go play golf with Coach," I replied quietly.

I fidgeted at the counter for a few minutes, grabbed my golf shoes, and went out to the garage. The garage door was open, and my dad's car was still warm from his drive home.

I tried to catch my breath.

What if my dad had come home and we were already in my room?

That was close. What was I thinking? I shook my hands vigorously trying to discard the shame and fear coursing through my body.

I heard Coach's truck before he turned into our driveway. I grabbed my clubs and threw them into the back before the tires stopped rolling. I jumped into the passenger seat and the words flew out of my mouth.

"My dad came home. We need to go. NOW."

Years later, with the help of a wise counselor, I came to understand how such secret relationships are tangled in a web of complexity. During that summer, as a way to survive the brainwashing, I started to believe I wanted the relationship. I convinced myself I held power and control over Coach. This inaccurate perception helped manage my confusion, but only dragged me further into the pit of shame.

40 // DON'T LEAVE

I stood a few yards away from Coach's truck in the parking lot near the practice range at TLV. He was agitated and intense, acting like *I* was the one betraying him.

"I don't want you to leave," he cried.

Mad and exasperated, my body started to shake. It took everything in me to control the volume of my voice so as not to draw attention towards us.

"What?" I asked through gritted teeth. "How can you even say that? I am leaving for college. Everything you helped me achieve—and now you don't want me to go?"

I had never seen him like this. I was surprised and confused. At the same time, I couldn't believe how selfish he was being. I closed my eyes and clenched my fists, willing myself to calm down.

"What are you going to do?" I hissed. "Leave your wife?"

His eyes dropped to the ground.

"You know I can't do that."

In a few days, I would be driving by myself from Idaho to San Jose, California, and this, *this*, was our goodbye. I was overwhelmed with different emotions, but all he was concerned about was his own.

His crying, almost groveling, felt so selfish. Days earlier he had suggested that we read the Bible together and then talk about it on the phone, him from Idaho and me from San Jose. I reminded him of that, even while feeling unsure of what he really meant or how it would work.

I lowered my voice and told him that leaving was really hard for me, too. Then came my tears. He couldn't comfort me because we were in a public parking lot. Someone might see us. We just stared at each other.

I finally gave him a quick hug, hopped in my car, and drove the short distance home.

After years of him basically dominating my life, something had started to break inside of me as I watched his tantrum. His world wasn't changing. He wasn't going to change. Yet, my whole world was changing, and it was evident he didn't care.

Fear entangled me. Fear of being found out. Fear of moving more than a thousand miles away from home. Fear of starting college, playing on an elite golf team, and fear that I wasn't going to be enough on my own.

41 // EVERYTHING IS OKAY

I gave my parents one last hug and climbed into my overly-stuffed Mazda 323 to start the drive to San Jose. I didn't think twice about driving over a thousand miles by myself. I'd been behind the wheel since I was eleven. I had it covered.

Besides, it was really only 850 miles to get to my half-sister Sheli's place in Sacramento on the first day. It was a quick stay, but I hoped now being only a few hours away from Sheli would help our tenuous relationship grow.

As I watched my parents waving in my rearview mirror as I pulled out of Twin Lakes Village, I was glad it wouldn't be long until I saw them again—a week later in Florida, at the PGA Junior Championship. It will be my last junior tournament before officially becoming a college student-athlete. But first I had to move into my freshman dorm room.

The terrain felt familiar as I headed southwest through Washington state, but I kept my eye on the Rand McNally map to make sure I followed the correct route. As I turned the steering wheel to take the exit toward Bend, Oregon, a wave of loneliness crashed over me.

My steely exterior seemed to crack; I had never been more aware of being alone. I steadied my focus on the road and the mountains ahead, turning up the radio for any kind of distraction from the growing emptiness inside me.

The mile markers swooshed by. Southern Oregon was nothing but the highway and mountains.

Under the noise of the speakers, my thoughts kept drifting to a book my dad had given me the Christmas before: *Meet My Head Coach*, by Fred Crowell.

I was a little shocked at the book. Dad never talked about faith or Jesus or God to my sister or me. I remember that he and Mom had answered some sort of an altar call once at an Amway event. But I never saw any evidence that Dad sought or even believed in God. When he remarried after my mother died, he did attend church. But he never talked about it.

Anyway, I had actually read the book, which was crazy because I wasn't one to read for fun. My Lutheran confirmation debacle years ago hadn't helped me understand God. But thinking of Him like a head coach made a little more sense. I didn't completely understand how to make Jesus my head coach, but I thought I could give it a go.

Cutting the radio, I breathed in the silence. Sheepishly, I looked around as if I might catch sight of God to point me toward the next step in the process. The book had mentioned something about saying a prayer to ask Jesus to come into my heart. So, I decided to try it. "Jesus, will you come into my heart?"

I didn't understand what I was saying, and I didn't know if I was saying it "right." I waited, but nothing earth-shattering happened. A few more minutes of silence, and still nothing. I turned the radio back on and kept driving, crossing the state line into California—my home for the next four years.

As I pulled into the dorm parking lot, I spotted Meredith, my friend and freshman teammate, waiting for me to arrive. Since my parents couldn't help me move, I was thankful for Meredith's familiar smile and willingness to pitch in. We went to work, unloading my car and schlepping all my belongings up to the fifth-floor room I'd been assigned. My roommate, a random student pick and non-athlete, hadn't moved in yet. I chose the bed by the window.

School was scheduled to begin the day after I returned from the tournament in Florida, so I decided to map things out before I left. I trekked around campus, locating where each class would be held. I had to settle one issue with a math class. The academic advisor put me in freshman math without my consultation, and that wasn't going to work for me. To stay on track with my goals, I needed to be in Calculus 1, but I hadn't been informed a math placement test was required.

"I'll do the test," I told the advisor, "and then I'll transfer classes." He agreed that I could try.

It was a full few days, but I felt fairly settled in my new home and was prepared to fly across the country and meet my parents for the PGA Junior Championship.

Florida's August humidity dripped off my skin within minutes of exiting the airport in Palm Beach. Rental car loaded down with clubs and suitcases, we headed toward PGA National Golf Course and our condo for the week. My white floppy hat was no match for the Florida sun, and my skin sizzled. It's amazing that none of us dropped from heat stroke.

With a free afternoon, my parents and I drove to the Atlantic Ocean. It was my first time dragging my feet through the soft, thick sand on the East Coast. I felt like a kid again, kicking the water playfully as I walked in search of seashells.

Then, I saw it from the corner of my eye. I didn't think it was anything at first, maybe just a piece of trash or driftwood. But, as I scooped away the sand, the salt water revealed an intricate, intact conch shell.

"Mom, Mom!" I yelled over to her. "Look at this! I found a conch shell."

We both beamed with joy—a treasure found in my mind and a souvenir to dampen another goodbye and the end of my junior golf career.

42 // A NEW ERA

Back on campus the following Monday, I stared in disbelief at the math placement results I'd been handed. Frustration tumbled off my tongue, but I refused to let my tears spill over. It couldn't be; I knew my math. How could I have missed advancing by only one question? I choked out a tense but controlled, "What do I do now?"

As I walked to the math building, I practiced my speech. I knocked once and stuck my head into the professor's office. I laid it all on the table, begging for her to consider my placement. "I need this class to start on track."

There was a flicker of pity in her eyes. "Okay," she said slowly, "if you can do this one problem from the book, right here in my office, I'll let you in. And, you can use the book for the formula."

Yes! A second chance. I sat down nervously, looking over the problem. I flipped the pages of the textbook for help. A half-hour passed and, one by one, my nerves frayed. Finally, I handed her the paper. The second hand of the clock echoed loudly in my brain as the professor reviewed my work. Then, she looked up with a smile. "I'll sign your transfer form."

With my classes put in order, I was ready to begin my freshman year.

Coach Gale was a no-nonsense retired colonel who informed us that we were responsible for both achieving good grades and preparing for our tournaments. "The van is leaving at 12:23 p.m.," he admonished. "Don't be late." And he wasn't joking around.

We all painfully watched a teammate running behind us and waving frantically, one minute late for the van call. Coach Gale just kept on driving, eyes forward on the road. We looked at each other in shock, and reality set in. There would be no hand-holding. Show up on time, never leave the ball below the hole, and practice on your own on the days we don't meet as a team. Coach Gale made his expectations clear.

I quickly learned Coach Gale had other quirks. He was a pacer. He never stopped moving when we were at practice. If we left our approach shot into the green short of the pin, then he would write an acronym on a ripped off piece of paper and stick it in the ground next to our ball. I'll just say it had at least one bad word in it. Coach Gale wore his emotions on his sleeve, never leaving us in doubt about how he was feeling.

The team was made up of two players from Sweden, four Californians, one from Hawaii, and me from Idaho. This was my freshman year. The players would change as I moved through my years.

It never crossed my mind what it would be like to play on a college golf team without our own practice facilities. The courses we played on three times a week were great, but practicing on the football scrimmage fields would not fly for me. I needed to find an alternative.

Randy, my swing instructor back in Idaho, recommended San Jose Municipal Golf Course, the "Muni." It was only four miles from campus and had a Henry-Griffitts golf club fitting system just like the clubs I have in my bag. Randy set me up with a lesson from one of the golf professionals, Bob, who had a similar teaching style to what I was used to.

I drove through a maze of streets to find the San Jose Muni. My clubs felt like a security blanket as I walked tentatively out to the practice range to find Bob. I kept my eye on each person I passed until a man turned and smiled. "You must be Tracy." He extended his hand.

I was thrilled with my lesson and hearing familiar language about my golf swing. When Bob said that he would love to keep working with me I was doubly excited. He suggested I go ask the head pro about practicing at the Muni.

The pro shop was small, dim, and crammed with merchandise. I've never liked introducing myself to strangers, much less asking for a favor. I nervously navigated around the racks to the back of the shop, locating the head pro's office.

Leaning back in his chair, he said, "Well, we don't normally do this, but how about you do a couple hours of work a month in exchange to practice and play when you need?"

"Yes, that could be great!" I said. "Thank you so much."

This was an arrangement I certainly could work with. It would mean avoiding the cost of a bucket of balls. I typically hit up to 300 balls in a session.

While the rest of my team practiced on SJSU's football fields, San Jose Muni would be my new home away from home.

I settled into my routine—class, practice, study, repeat.

43 // UNTRACEABLE

The phone rang twice. Silence followed. I knew it was him.

Thankfully my roommate was gone. I dialed his number, using my AT&T calling card for the charges. It barely rang before I heard, "Hello." Then, "I miss you."

"I miss you, too," I responded half-heartedly.

"I'm going to come to your tournament."

I had earned a spot on the top-5 for our first tournament of the fall semester in Vancouver, Washington.

"Okay." My cheeks flushed. "That's only a few weeks away."

"If I get there early, can I take you to dinner?"

I gulped and squeaked out a reply. "I'll ask Coach Gale if I can."

We had rehearsed this drill before I left Idaho. Every week, he called and hung up after a couple of rings. I called back using a calling card, making it untraceable on his phone records. He sent me money to pay for our calls.

During our conversations, I mostly listened to him. I couldn't think of much to say. But he was a connection to home, easing my homesickness. For more than four years, he helped me achieve and excel. I wouldn't be the athlete that I was without him.

I also hated the calls. We rarely talked about God or discussed the Bible like he had suggested before I moved. The weight of our secret was drowning me; I felt trapped and powerless.

I can't imagine, now, how this still seventeen-year-old version of me was able to navigate this abusive relationship, on top of handling the transition to being a collegiate student athlete. Back then, breaking my silence was impossible. My world would have imploded, and I had too much to lose. But with every passing week, away from him and our routine, the realization was growing that this relationship was not okay.

My heart breaks for how alone I felt in the process.

44 // DISTRACTIONS

The yellow stitching popped off the royal blue garment bag: San Jose State University. As I packed for my first collegiate golf tournament, I thought, *How in the world did I qualify, as a freshman, in the number one position?* Shaking my head, I packed away four days of uniforms and essentials. I did not feel ready. I felt homesick, though, and I knew my parents would be there. Coach would be there, too.

Our direct flight into Portland, Oregon, descended toward the runway. The beauty of the Columbia River, Mount Hood, and Mount St. Helens saluted me back home to the Northwest. As soon as we landed, we packed our large travel golf bags and suitcases into the van and jumped in. Coach Gale headed toward Interstate 5. We crossed the Columbia River from Oregon into Vancouver, Washington, and navigated to Royal Oaks Country Club. Once we arrived, we were all ready for food. Our golf team were champion eaters.

When we finished with our practice round, Coach Gale dropped me and two of other teammates off at where we would be staying, in the home of a family named Thun. We were still getting to know one another, but we were a good fit for the three guest bedrooms while our other two teammates were set up at another house on the golf course. Our house rested by the ninth tee box. I hung back for a moment and approached Coach Gale.

"My old coach is coming to town for the tournament. Would you be okay if he takes me out to dinner tonight?"

"Sure, just make sure you get back early to get ready for tomorrow," he replied.

For the rest of the late afternoon, I could hardly concentrate. I tried to act cool, as if it were normal for my high school coach to drive six hours to watch me play my first college tournament. It had been only just over a month since I'd seen him. Part of me missed him, part of me was nearly sick to my stomach with nerves, part of me wished he wouldn't come. The denial of reality was still there. I was still so young. In one month, I would turn eighteen.

When Coach arrived, I climbed in his car, shaky and uncertain. All through an awkward dinner, I couldn't not think about why he really had come. I knew what he wanted. After paying for the meal, he drove us to his hotel room. Eventually I finally noticed the glowing clock on the nightstand said it was almost ten o'clock. Coach Gale was going to kill me.

Coach drove me back to the Thuns'. The whole way back, I stared out of the car window, silently scolding myself for allowing it to happen again.

I opened the front door like a mouse, eager to not wake anyone. I tiptoed up the stairs to my room, brushed my teeth, and fell into bed, exhausted. My thoughts punished me until I fell asleep.

"You were out late last night," one of my teammates quipped the next morning, greeting me with raised eyebrows.

I stopped in my tracks on the threshold of the kitchen. My red face and incoherent words betrayed me. "We were at dinner and lost track of time."

But they knew. I was caught.

They moved onto other conversation—how to work the toaster, what to expect at the tournament. Meanwhile, my thoughts spun. *What are they thinking? What do they think about me?*

My parents showed up in time for the tournament. I almost knocked my mom over with a big hug. I gave my dad a quick embrace and then hustled to the range to warm up.

I was a mess. I needed my nerves to calm down. As I walked down the first fairway, I saw my parents and Coach trekking off to the side together.

My first round went poorly. Most holes ended in three-putts. I wanted to blame it on freshman jitters, but that wasn't the cause. Every time I saw Coach walking along with my parents, I pictured a billboard with our secret plastered on it. Thankfully he only stayed to watch the first round, but it was enough to fray my nerves.

After two disappointing rounds, I gave myself a stern pep talk. I needed to let the onlookers and the previous rounds go. I worked through my warm-up routine. *It's a new day. No distractions. I can do this.*

I looked up and eyed my final putt: downhill, six feet away. My whole body shook. "This is going to be a very fast putt, so don't be too aggressive,"

I muttered.

I barely moved the putter head back before releasing. The ball bumped forward and descended toward the cup, rolling in slow-motion. It stopped one inch shy of the cup. I collapsed into a squat in disbelief before tapping it in for par.

Exhausted but giddy, I walked to the scorer's tent to sign my scorecard. I didn't want to screw up by forgetting to sign it and be disqualified. Every detail matters in golf.

My scorecard was filled with six circles around my birdies, and a double circle around my eagle. Against the few squares around my bogies, my score added up to 70, four under par.

My team won the tournament, and I moved up to seventh overall in the individual standing.

Coach Gale grabbed me into a big hug. "Way to come back today."

Later, I heard him say to a reporter, "She's going to be a winner. She'll have a lot of rounds like that this year."

45 // TREMORS

The massive Bay Area earthquake in 1989 rolled the ground under my feet nearly two feet up and down, knocking me to the ground. Parked cars were shuffled around like toys. Trees tilted. Tiles flew. It scared me but I survived.

My golf teammates rallied around each other in the days after the October quake and under Coach Gale's guidance. I saw that I had a group I could rely on. I was homesick, but I was handling it and beginning to find my stride and adjust to college life.

The all-you-can-eat cereal at the dorm cafeteria was the bomb. The rest of the food was sufficient. I did notice that my clothes stopped fitting as well. That frustrated me. I refused to believe that the freshman fifteen was real but I felt fat.

To top it off, my period was missing for two months. I had heard similar stories from other freshmen girls. Then, it hit me.

On one of our calls, I mentioned my fears to Coach. He basically said nothing helpful. I understood I was on my own and I hung up feeling even more alone. I had no desire to talk to him anymore. I turned to a teammate, Meredith, who had become a friend.

"What am I going to do?" I vacantly stared at her, too scared to cry.

"We will go to the pregnancy center to get you tested. Okay?" she said.

Her kindness forced a breath out of me, "Okay."

Meredith stayed with me for a few nights. My roommate was gone, and I didn't want to be alone.

The dimly lit, sterile pregnancy center sucked up all my breath when we walked through the threshold, leaving me light-headed. I spoke to the receptionist, the words tumbled out of my mouth, but nothing registered in my mind.

Was this real?

After filling out the paperwork, I waited with Meredith. The tick of the second hand echoed around the room. I was there, but not really there.

"What am I going to do if I'm pregnant?" A mere whisper rasped out with my shallow breath.

Meredith put her arm around me just as a voice called, "Tracy, you can come with me now." I looked at Meredith. Her eyes assured me she would be right there when I returned.

I peed into a cup, shaking and cold. I slid it back to the nurse. Then we waited.

The second hand teased us again. We waited, and waited, and waited. My mind was spinning. *What am I going to do? I can't be pregnant. I'm a freshman in college. How would I tell my parents? I can't tell my parents. This can't be happening.*

Then, my agony was vanquished. The test came back negative. I looked at Meredith, and my tears finally came.

The next time I talked with Coach, I said simply, "I finally found a spot." My relief at the sight of menstrual blood was muted by the numbness I still felt. He understood what I meant, and we never mentioned it again.

46 // ENDING IT

As I stared out into the sky at 30,000 feet, I imagined hugging my mom. I longed for her warmth. I envisioned the two of us baking chocolate chip cookies. My heart hurt thinking about home.

I had made it through my first college semester. The months away felt like a rollercoaster ride: the uphill battle with my confidence, the acclimation to the speed of college classes and dorm life, the ups and down of my golf game, and the exhilaration of my two top-five individual finishes. I never played or practiced as much as I did my first semester at college. I was ready for a break from my golf clubs.

A whole month home. A month for holidays, family, and my hometown. Meredith was coming from the Bay Area for several days as well. We planned to watch my alma mater girls' basketball team play their last game before Christmas break.

The game was being played against one of my old rival schools on their court. When I walked into the gym, it felt familiar, like another piece of home. But it terrified me too. I would see Coach. The possible pregnancy still pulsed in the pit of my stomach.

Back when we had been on that call about the pregnancy scare, I had heard a click in the background. It turns out that Coach's wife had picked up the other receiver—accidentally or intentionally, I don't know—and had been listening to a part of our conversation. Coach later told me she had asked him what I was talking about when I said I "found a spot." He deftly explained it by saying I had found a spot to attend church.

I remembered feeling tightness and fear that we were caught. He assured me that she believed him and she didn't ask anything further. My gut remembered the nausea I felt.

Meredith and I sat quietly in the bleachers. It felt surreal to watch high school girls basketball. Nothing was different, yet everything was. A year ago, I ran the show. A year ago, it was me that Coach was yelling at. Watching him now was like an out-of-body experience. I felt so detached from it—and from him.

A conviction had been building all semester—maybe even starting with our painful goodbye scene, or just the consequence of time and distance—that I couldn't go on pretending anymore. Something needed to change. Being away from him helped me feel like an outside observer. I realized our secret relationship was a lie.

The next day, I woke up early. Snapshots of the game were dancing in my head. Meredith was up too. I asked her for a favor as I left the house. "Tell my mom I had an errand to run."

I found the side door left ajar. I slid into the shadows of the gym, the latch clicking behind me. I followed the wall toward the boys locker room. My heart pounded, and my breath was shallow. *I can do this. I want to do this. I have to do this.*

Stenchy odor wafted into my face as I entered. I called out, "Hey, are you in here?"

He stepped out, backlit by his office's dim light. He grabbed me and kissed me, but I pulled away. Something different stirred inside me, a resistance. He tilted his head and asked if I was okay.

NO. I'm not okay.

I stopped his movements and said, "No, I don't want to do this anymore."

He stared back at me, stunned.

"No more. I almost lost everything a couple months ago. This is over."

I clenched my body, fighting back my tears. I could tell his heart was racing too. He took a few deep breaths and stroked my arms, frowning.

"Okay . . . okay," he mumbled.

When he pulled me to him in a hug, I let him. He whispered, "Are you sure?"

I didn't say anything. I just stepped out of his arms and looked at him.

"I'll see you at open gym?" he asked.

"Maybe."

I ran out of the darkness. Punching the gas pedal, I clenched the steering wheel and tore out of the parking lot.

Breathe.

You did it.

47 // ASKING FORGIVENESS

Three weeks whizzed by. Christmas blurred into the New Year. I decided to stay home instead of returning to San Jose for the three-week January semester. I could enjoy my own bed, the warmth of our pellet stove, and the blanket of snow. I could also participate in open gym at the high school for pick-up basketball.

The familiar squeak of shoes across the gym floor perked me up. I tore off my coat and grabbed a ball. The leather rolled against my hands with each bounce. I tossed the ball up with a backward spin, sending it into flight. The subsequent swoosh pumped my blood. *Let's play some basketball.*

I knew Coach would be there. I hadn't seen him since I found the courage to say *no more* a couple weeks prior. We hadn't spoken by phone either.

He grabbed my arm as I was leaving. He asked to come by the house, for "closure." My breath caught high in my throat. Seconds passed before I mumbled, "Okay, I guess."

As uncomfortable as the visit made me feel, I was certain I wasn't hoping for "one last time" with Coach or "testing" the situation. I believed I felt resolved that the wrong relationship was over and done with, and things (like playing open gym) could go back to "normal." We could go on with our lives.

Mom and Dad were still at work when I came home. Our dog, Muffin, and I paced the living room carpet, waiting for Coach to arrive. Our heads cocked simultaneously at the sound of his car door. I peered down at Muffin for reassurance. "I'm good. I can do this."

I let him in the house. We shared an awkward hug and sat on the couch. I scooched away, making sure there was space between us. He started talking, and I disassociated. My body was there, but my mind left the room, until I heard, "We need to ask God for forgiveness."

I snapped back to the moment, confused. My thoughts accelerated, trying to make sense of his words. Christianity was new to me. The whole "relationship with God" thing still felt foreign. I had already bought into the idea that I was complicit and as guilty as he was. What was he trying to accomplish by talking about forgiveness?

"Why don't we both pray? I'll go first," he said confidently.

When he was done, I copied his prayer, then looked up, slapped on some confidence, and smiled. I sat guarded as he got up. He turned back with a grin as he was leaving. "See you at the next open gym."

Looking back, I see now that he was controlling the narrative to protect himself. By making me feel as responsible as he was, he was solidifying the belief that we both had to keep this relationship a secret.

When I ran into him again during break, he reinforced his strategy: "I hope we can still be friends." I didn't really know what he meant. But I guessed that that was why we prayed together. If God forgives, we can leave our relationship in the past. If God forgives us, it must all be okay.

A couple of weeks later, I walked with my mom to the departure gate. My stomach tightened, but I needed to return to school. I hugged her, not wanting to let go. "I love you, Mom. Everything's going to be okay." If she suspected anything amiss, she never asked.

I held back my tears, but the dam burst halfway down the jet bridge.

Dad and me at Twin Lakes Village, Idaho, waiting to kick off July 4th festivities with our trumpets (c. 1982).

The grandparents I grew up with: Earl and Lorraine Carroll, known to us as PāPā and MāMā. Easter 1988.

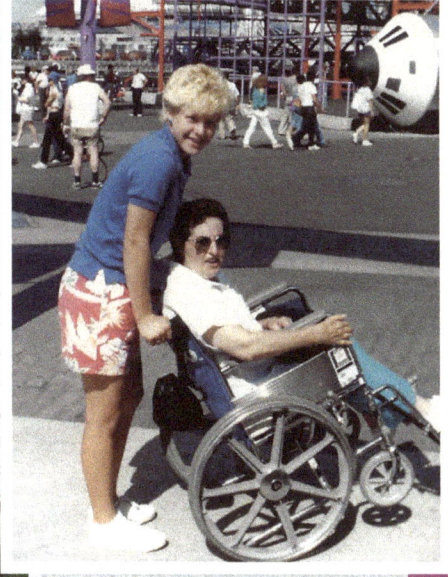

Freewheeling with MāMā all over the 1986 World's Fair in Vancouver, BC, Canada.

From left: Me, Mom, Dad, and Debbie, on Easter 1988.

My varsity basketball photo (1988-89), the year we won state. I was tournament MVP, and A-2 Player of the Year.

My high school senior photo. I was surprised at being named 1989 class valedictorian.

The four senior athletes, graduating together after years of friendship and winning Idaho A2 Girl's State Championship.

Winning the 1989 Women's Western Junior Golf Championship, my first national junior championship victory.

PART THREE:
THE AFTERMATH

48 // BREAKING 70

The Arizona sun breached my untanned skin, warming me from the inside out. It was somehow already April of my freshman year. After two days of play in Tempe at the Lady Sun Devil Invitational, Arizona State had a 17-stroke lead over Arizona. My San Jose State teammates and I felt Coach Gale's rising discontentment, ever aware that we were getting our butts whipped sitting 30 shots behind the leader.

The links-style Karsten Golf Course, where the tournament was being held, was nestled on the outskirts of the Arizona State campus, with an impressive football stadium as its backdrop. Under the cloudless sky, the desert rocks reflected the unforgiving sun and I found myself squinting most of the day to protect my baby-blue eyes—not quite able to take in everything around me.

I bantered with my inner voice, trying to deflect the monologue that chided me for my first two rounds of 76–75. I'd been persistently working on my game, especially my short game as Coach Dana had instructed me to. But, all the pieces hadn't come together in one round yet.

I had been keeping our seniors on their toes, even taking one of the top two spots in our positioning on the team several times, but that infamous 70 barrier still eluded me. I could almost taste it—in fact, I had tasted its faint trace many times at the beginning of a round—but I couldn't bring myself to the strong finish I needed. Moving into the Top 20 nationally ranked was still in reach, but I wanted, no, I needed, to break 70.

Coach Gale's morning pep talk still rang in my ears. "We may not be able to win this tournament, but we don't quit until the last putt drops," he exhorted us. "Use this round as another stepping stone on our journey to the NCAA Championship."

I felt fairly positive about the whole thing. We really had nothing to lose, playing for second place—barring ASU completing the round without catastrophe.

Coming off a bogey, I calculated my yardage on the par-three seventh in a fluster. I felt my stomach clench. Coach Gale approached me with an update on the wind's behavior, and his presence calmed me back to composure. okay, *Tracy, come on*, my inner voice spurred. *Get focused and sharpen things up.* A deep breath.

I made my best shot of the day.

I picked my ball out of the hole for a birdie. I hit four more fairways in a row, scrambled to save par twice, and made my second two on the par-three 12th. There were just six holes ahead of me. How many birdies could I make?

Par. Birdie. Birdie. Electricity surged through me. I was three under par with three holes left. Coach Gale found me again, joining me on the walk down the 16th fairway. He was giddy because the luck seemed to have spread—everyone was playing top-of-their game. I had grown accustomed to his nervous mannerisms, which grounded me. I couldn't help but laugh.

After missing the green on the par-five 17th, I fought against tension in my hands. "Focus. Breathe. You've got this," I repeated to myself, a mantra of concentration. I grabbed my ball out of the cup and, after a solid up-and-down for par, found a little skip in my walk to the 18th.

One more, and I've done it. Focus. Breathe.

Fairway—check. Green—a dot for the stats. Two putts remained between me and my first 69.

I looked up to see my teammates, Coach Dana, and Coach Gale huddled together off the back of the green. Coach Gale paced back and forth, as usual, waiting for the determining putts. Seeing the group of smiles encouraged me.

Minutes later, I was barreled down with hugs and high-fives. My first 69. I did it.

And the cherry on top of that warm April day in 1990: Our team shot both our best-ever team score of 283 and the low round of the tournament.

49 // HOME FOR SUMMER

My bedroom was mostly the same, but home felt different this time. *I* felt different. Nine months ago—the fall of 1989—might as well have been nine years ago. So much can happen in such a short time span. I finished my first year of college. I was ranked twentieth in the nation; I was Second Team All-American; and I had five top-ten NCAA Division I finishes to my name.

I also had a "real" boyfriend. By this point, I had buried the relationship with Coach deep in the recesses of my soul. I believed I had moved on. It was time to focus on *my* life. What I didn't understand was that the hidden secret was like a slow internal bleed.

My new boyfriend, Doug, who happened to have the same last name as me, had wonderful parents. They seamlessly filled a role as my "college parents." They were also kind enough to store my belongings in their garage for summer break. I intentionally planned to play a tournament in Northern California midsummer just so I could visit the Hanson family.

After settling in at home, it was time to get a "real" job. I knew it was going to cut into my summer and my practice time, but I needed to make money. I began working at the TLV Golf Course behind the counter collecting green fees, picking the practice range, and helping golfers get off the first tee. I did the grunt work too, prepping the golf carts before dawn, washing them, and putting them away at night. But I was thankful for the job, and especially for my boss who allowed me to take time off for summer tournaments.

My first event was the U.S. Women's Amateur Public Links Championship in Fort Collins, Colorado. The northern Colorado mountains were beautiful on the western horizon and made our Idaho mountains look puny. Two weeks prior, I won the local qualifier to secure my spot in the national tournament. The Public Links is "a championship for golfers who played on public courses, as members of private clubs were barred from entry," as defined by the USGA. I loved my public golf roots and I wanted to win this championship.

I didn't play my best in the first two days of stroke play, but thankfully well enough to make it into the match-play rounds. After winning my first three matches, I made it to the semi-finals. Two matches stood between me and holding the championship trophy.

I felt nauseous while I warmed up on the range for my semi-final match. This is a big deal. I am on the national stage.

The day didn't end as I had hoped. We dueled it out to the last few holes, and then my tee shot off the sixteenth tee hit a fairway bunker rake, which sent my ball deep into the bunker. I lost the match after making a double bogey. The pang of disappointment punched me in the gut, but I was very encouraged with the way I played all week.

Between work, practice, and tournaments, the rest of my summer schedule flew by. I had a fun week in San Jose visiting Doug and his parents, Les and Lynn Hanson, and playing in a Players West Tour event where I finished second to my San Jose State teammate, Pat Hurst. A rare feat for two amateurs to take first and second in a professional event.

I went to a few open gyms and played some golf with Coach. I figured it was okay to be around him and just be friends. It was all behind us and I told myself we were both moving on.

Before long there were only a few weeks left before I drove back to campus. Sophomore year was fast approaching.

50 // **THE NEXT STEP**

It was dark in this corner of campus. Honestly, I wasn't sure that I'd ever actually walked in this area before. *Was I in the wrong place?* I stood frozen, staring at the giant steel door in front of me for an eternity. It felt like an eternity, at least. I didn't want to touch the cold steel. *There are people on the other side of the door that I don't know,* I thought. *I can't do this. Just turn around and leave, Tracy.*

In the split-second I tried to escape, three "happy faces" appeared out of nowhere. "Hey!" one exclaimed. "Are you here for the Campus Crusade for Christ and Athletes in Action meeting?"

"Uh, yeah," I stammered. "I think so. I wasn't sure if this was the right building." Their exuberance whisked me through the scary door where I found a new and much different world.

Four months ago, as my freshman year was ending in May, I had checked the box on an information card indicating that I wanted more information about Athletes in Action (AIA). Now back on campus for my sophomore year that fall, the AIA crew tracked me down. Up to that point, I don't think I even knew what the word "ministry" meant, and I certainly didn't make any attempts to connect with any sort of Christian student organization during my first year at San Jose. Instead, I found solace in producing high grades in class and low scores on the golf course.

However, I had begun to ponder things. If I was serious about the whole "God thing" then I needed a next step. Thankfully, I survived that first Campus Crusade for Christ (CRU) and AIA meeting. For the rest of my college years, I continued attending weekly meetings whenever my schedule allowed. I even found one of my two roommates for my last two years of college in that room behind the scary door.

The other students and athletes involved in CRU and AIA became my college family. Some were a little too over-the-top happy, I thought, but I experienced a goodness radiating from the group that felt *different*. It went beyond good grades or good golf—I found people who genuinely cared about me.

Over the next three school years, I learned what I named *Christianity 101*: how to read the Bible, the concept of a quiet time (spending time with God by reading, praying, and journaling), the importance of being a part of a church community, and discipleship/leadership training (how to share my "testimony" and the gospel). By far, the worst activity for this introvert was passing out little brochures about Jesus Christ to random people on the street. CRU and AIA offered me new guardrails for how I spent my time and desired to live my life—most of them good, some less so.

In the fall of my sophomore year I started meeting with the CRU female staff member. As we spent time together she made me feel as if she truly wanted to get to know me and help me grow. I started to feel safe with her. I'd been hiding what happened in high school for so long, and felt so dirty and damaged, I wanted something to change. I began to have an urge to tell someone. I felt I needed to confess my sin.

It made sense for me to tell her, but I was terrified of what she'd think. What would she say? What would she do?

I stuttered and mumbled, but I finally choked out the story. *I am going to puke*, I thought. It took everything in me to hold it together. The staff member was still young—barely past her mid-twenties. She looked at me with kindness in her eyes. "God loves you," she reminded me. She suggested we pray together; I could ask for forgiveness. But it would take decades to understand this is not what I needed at that point in time.

I jumped right into what was suggested. I made the CRU and AIA meetings, discipleship training, attending church, and the AIA retreats a high priority. It felt so good to be part of something besides golf. And learning to do the "right thing" as a young Christian wasn't too different from the self-discipline and sacrifices required of an athlete.

As I worked my way through the discipleship training materials, the CRU campus staff leader asked if I would share my testimony at one of our weekly meetings. My heart quickened. I still hated speaking in front of groups, and now I was being asked to share about what my life was like before I started following Jesus, how I came to say yes to following Jesus, and what had happened since. I wanted to say "no," but I said "yes."

The night came and I felt more nervous than any golf tournament had ever made me. Leading worship was a guest gospel-music choir, the first I'd ever encountered. Standing with the singers behind me, I took the mic and glanced down at my notes. Right in the middle of my first sentence, a loud "Praise the Lord" erupted from behind and startled me. I began again. In mid-sentence, I glanced over my shoulder. Hands were raised and smiles stretched a mile wide. Bursts of praise continued as I stumbled my way through the story I was trying to share.

When I sat down, I was exhausted. But *I did it*—I shared what the CRU leaders called my testimony with the whole group. As a good student, I used all the right jargon. I talked about how, growing up, I sought approval through my sports performance. I also said I was learning how much God loves me and that He forgives all of my sins. I made sure I added how important the CRU and AIA group had been to my new spiritual growth and how I wanted to live my life for God's glory.

I decided not to talk about my high school "relationship." It didn't feel appropriate.

It's bittersweet for me to look back on those years with CRU and AIA. Without a doubt, I grew in my understanding of who God is and His unfailing love for me. I experienced good friendships and new forms of fun. I became a Christian athlete, and I was proud to hold that title. But I also found another place to perform—to perform for Jesus, to say the right things, to hide my true feelings, and to lock up my pain and confusion. I rode the emotional rollercoaster of good and bad decisions.

God changed the trajectory of my life in those years. It would take another two decades, however, for me to find the courage to enter the *real story*.

51 // A YEAR OF FIRSTS

I won my first college tournament halfway around the world in Japan at the Shiseido Cup International Collegiate, where teams from sixteen different nations compete in a three-day event. My five-foot-seven frame with short blond hair and blue eyes was a sight to behold on that golf course. I was an outsider in every way!

I found solace with the club in my hand, and something clicked on the mountainous course. My drives were long, and my short game was refined. I finished two under par for three rounds and won by six shots. I couldn't stop smiling—until I had to give a victory speech.

That first taste of victory whet my appetite for more, and thankfully, I didn't have to wait long. Less than a month later, I dominated the Scarlet Course—a monster of a golf course—at The Ohio State University for my second win in the fall of my sophomore year. Our top-ranked team was on fire.

The next spring, in 1991, we traveled to New Orleans for the LSU Invitational in Baton Rouge. Most of us, me included, had never been to Louisiana. I didn't like the spicy gumbo, but the beignets were delicious.

While Bourbon Street wasn't my scene, the Fairwood Country Club suited me just right. We sloshed around the rain-drenched course with a thirty-four-stroke team victory, and I finished the third round with a personal best, six-under 66.

Coach Gale called it, "The most perfect round of college golf I've ever seen played."

I extended my streak of par rounds and better to seven and won the Big West Conference Championship by fourteen strokes in Las Cruces, New Mexico. If we could have pulled off a win in May at the NCAA Championship at the Scarlet Course, my season would have been complete.

We were so close! We had the win in our hands until our team disintegrated on the last nine of the last round. We lost in a play-off against UCLA.

It was an exciting year marked by many firsts and personal bests, including being the number two ranked player in the NCAA Division I golf rankings. Coach Gale started calling me a diamond in the rough.

After packing up my apartment, I was ready to return to North Idaho and turn my attention to the upcoming summer tournaments.

52 // A SUMMER OF SUCCESS

The summer of 1991 started off with a bang. The table for the biggest golf day of my career was set at the 1991 U.S. Women's Public Links in Charlottesville, Virginia.

I earned medalist honors (low finisher in first two rounds of stroke play) and scorched through one match at a time until I met a player named Carrie Wood in the finals, which was normally a thirty-six-hole match. But rain delays at the Birdwood Golf Course pushed both the semi-final and the final matches into Sunday.

I handily defeated another competitor, Nicole Jeray, eight-and-seven in the morning semi-final match. But my confidence went awry early in the round against Carrie. Standing on the seventh hole three down, my internal pep talk was sharp. *I can do this.* Feeling my feet back on the ground, I birdied the seventh, ninth, thirteenth, and fifteenth holes. Remembering my birdie putt on thirteen gave me the confidence to stand over the five-foot par putt on the eighteenth hole and make it to win the match *and* the championship. And just like that, I was a national champion with a coveted USGA trophy and gold medal in hand.

The victory also gained me a berth into the U.S. Women's Open at Colonial Country Club in Fort Worth, Texas. I had never tried to qualify for the Women's Open before because I didn't feel ready. I still felt like a small fish in the very big pond of the women's amateur golf world, but I had momentum and my excitement oozed out of me as I made my plans for my first U.S. Women's Open.

One major detail needed to be solved immediately. I was required to have a caddy to play at the Open. My dad really wanted to caddy. At this point in my expanding golf career, he had had no involvement other than being a spectator. I didn't feel it was the best decision for Dad to caddy, but he wanted to and saving money mattered. I would at least have someone familiar with me too. I told him he will carry the bag and I will do everything else. Meaning, I would get my yardages and make my course management decisions. Other than a few moments of irritation, we made it work.

Playing on the Ladies Professional Golf Tour (LPGA) was my ultimate dream destination. The U.S. Open was my first time inside the ropes (each fairway is lined by stakes and ropes creating a boundary between players and fans during play) with these professional female golfers instead of watching from afar. The Colonial Golf Club, a coveted golf course and favorite of Ben Hogan's, commanded attention and respect. The narrow fairways required accuracy, not distance.

The Texas heat and slow rounds were just as much of an obstacle as the greens. I played respectable rounds the first two days (75–76) to make the cut by one. I didn't have a chance at winning the tournament, but I was in the race for the low-amateur medal. Vicki Goetze and I were back and forth. After the final round, I edged Vicki out by one stroke with my two weekend rounds of even-par 71.

Then I found myself standing at the awards ceremony right next to the U.S. Women's Open Champion, Meg Mallon. A surreal feeling is an understatement. The expansive crowd clapped and cheered as I received my USGA medal. I couldn't stop shaking and smiling.

My U.S. Women's Public Links win also qualified me to play in my first USGA U.S. Women's Amateur at Prairie Dunes in Hutchinson, Kansas. It was the last golf match on my summer schedule before heading back to college. It's hard to believe that such an iconic golf course existed amidst those vast plains and farmland. Prairie Dunes was truly idyllic with narrow fairways, undulating greens, and heather grass ready to swallow an errant shot. I drew the reigning NCAA Individual Champion, Annika Sorenstam, for the first round of match play. I played hard but eventually lost on the nineteenth hole.

I gained invaluable experience over the summer, and I was determined to keep the momentum going into my junior year at SJSU.

53 // A DIRT DARE

"I dare you to eat your divot for twenty dollars."

Was Nicole serious? There we were, during practice at Los Altos Country Club, laughing and teasing another teammate, Ninni, about the twenty-dollar debt she owed Nicole for accepting a dare to eat a spoonful of wasabi. (I have no idea how we came up with these things. I also have no idea why we were discussing this on the golf course.) Suddenly, Nicole turned to me and the girls started teasing me about my frugalness.

It was common knowledge that I was frugal. Extremely frugal. I preferred to label it as "fiscally responsible." I stretched out my monthly scholarship per diem to the very last nickel to cover housing, food, and gas. Frivolous spending wasn't an option, and having any extra money in my wallet was a rare reality. Was eating dirt worth twenty dollars?

"And you have to chew and swallow it," Nicole added.

A long silence hung in the air as I considered the pros and cons of the challenge. I have never been one to back down from a bet, and this one felt like it was an easy tradeoff. What's a little divot dirt going to hurt? Twenty dollars was a lot of money for a poor college student.

I picked up the three-inch by two-inch chunk of grassy dirt and started eating. I didn't let myself think about the bugs, pesticide, and who knows what else was in there. I wasn't allowed any water until I had completely swallowed it. After much hand-waving and gagging, the piece of dirt sat itself in my stomach like a lead weight. I opened my empty mouth and stuck out my chocolate-brown tongue while the girls laughed in amazement.

For a few moments of disgust, I was twenty dollars richer and some belly laughs stronger. I have no regrets.

54 // UPS AND DOWNS

We were the number one nationally ranked team during the 1991–92 season, and we were out for blood.

Even after a strong season in the fall of my junior year, the sting of losing the NCAA Championship the spring before was still fresh. We were not going to let it slip away again.

I had a few more wins under my belt, and my confidence on the golf course continued to grow as my play improved. My proudest victory was just down the road at the California Collegiate Tournament at Stanford University. It was a marathon—eighteen holes the first day followed by thirty-six holes the second day.

Stanford was touted as the "big kid" in the Bay Area by a variety of sports outlets. Beating them on their home course provoked extra incentive for us SJSU Spartans. I struggled with my putting in the second round, but my bookend scores of sixty-nine and sixty-eight led our team to a fourteen-stroke victory, and my eight-under par tied the course record. We didn't just win, we whooped them. Giddy with pride, Coach Gale drove the forty minutes back to campus and treated us to a feast at Original Joe's Italian restaurant.

Golf continued to be all-consuming. Nationals was just around the corner at the Arizona State University Karsten Golf Course—the same course where I shot my first sixty-nine as a freshman. I was also busy preparing for play on a larger stage immediately following the NCAAs: in England.

Back in early January, I knew the USGA Curtis Cup selection committee had started putting together the American team, and I anxiously waited to hear if I was one of the lucky players selected. The Curtis Cup was (and still is) the most prestigious team trophy for women amateur golfers from the U.S., Great Britain, and Ireland. Never in my wildest dreams did I imagine playing on our country's team. Yet, my U.S. Women's Public Links Championship and low amateur score in the U.S. Open piqued the committee's interest.

It was the evening of January 31, and I sat disheartened at the kitchen counter nervously crunching my cereal. Cereal is one of my favorite nighttime comfort snacks. Time was running out. Would I get the call?

At nine p.m., the phone rang. "Hello," I answered calmly, and with no indication I had been anxiously waiting all day and practically leapt out of my skin when I heard the phone.

The U.S. team captain, Judy, introduced herself and shared the news. "You have been selected to represent the United States at the Curtis Cup, would you like to accept?"

"Yes, yes," I replied, trying desperately to sound professional. Meanwhile the force of my fist pumping knocked me off balance and almost tipped my stool over. "Absolutely, I would like to accept. Thank you for selecting me."

I couldn't believe it. I was going to represent my country at the 1992 Curtis Cup. But before I could spend too much time thinking about this great honor, I had to give my full attention to the fast-approaching NCAA Championship.

The Arizona sun beat down on us relentlessly. Phoenix is hot in late May and our team was tired. We played strong the first three days of the NCAA tournament, and we were well positioned on the fourth and final day to bring home a third NCAA title for the SJSU women's golf program. Unlike last year, our team would not collapse. We couldn't. We were determined to push the golf gremlins out and take our confidence to the finish; this was our time.

Our team's five-stroke lead with two holes left shrank to one stroke. The pressure was mounting. After many seasons of building trust and rapport, Coach Gale's presence helped to encourage and steady us, something we needed more than ever in this moment.

Standing in the left rough on the seventeenth hole, I knew I needed to play it safe and hit my approach shot away from the pin, but still give myself room for a birdie putt. The Arizona player took a more aggressive line that cost her a triple-bogey. Her mistake coupled with my birdie putt gave us a four-stroke lead, and the chance for my teammate Lisa and me to finish the eighteenth hole breathing easy.

Coach Gale paced the hillside on the backside of the green and I had to physically hold him back from rushing the green while Lisa's final par putt dropped in the hole. The rest of our team spun the lid off a water cooler and patiently waited to dump it on Coach Gale. Hugs, laughter, and high-fives filled the air around us as Coach Gale's pride dripped with the water over his head. We won! A full team effort as we took turns holding the NCAA Championship trophy.

I didn't have long to celebrate, though. Less than twenty-four hours later, Vicki Goetze, the NCAA Individual Champion, and I took an early-morning flight from Arizona to travel all day and night to England. There we met up with our Curtis Cup Team at the Royal Liverpool Golf Course in the seaside town of Hoylake.

I was exhausted, scared, and not at all looking forward to wearing my pleated skirt uniform at the opening ceremony. My sweet mom pinned every single pleat so I wouldn't have to iron it. When I pulled it out of my suitcase, Vicki howled with laughter at my mom's painstaking effort to keep my skirt wrinkle-free.

Walking the fairways at Royal Liverpool, I experienced golf in an entirely new way. It was like playing pinball to avoid the deep pot bunkers, and the large greens were undulating but slow. The golf ball rolled along the firm fairways crowded with fans all supporting their British golfers. Our captain, Judy, paired me with Carol Semple-Thompson, who was the most steady and accomplished player on the team. She helped settle my nerves as we played our alternate shot match, winning with a couple holes left to play.

The travel and exhaustion caught up with me. I woke up with a cold and a tight back on the last day of play—the single matches. All competitors played head-to-head. I drew Catriona Matthew, against whom I had played in some college tournaments. Now she was on her home turf and playing exceptionally well. I was a mess, and my confidence disappeared with the morning tide.

We lost the Curtis Cup. I felt like a big failure to my team. The players from Great Britain rubbed salt in our wounds, blaring "We Are the Champions" on the bus ride back to the hotel. I felt like a small goldfish trying to survive in a vast ocean.

Our England tour continued into the next week. We navigated the train system and worked our way to the southern end of the country for the British Amateur Championship, where I somewhat redeemed myself by winning one match.

Vicki and I stayed with a family who allowed us to use their Land Rover to go exploring. What were they thinking? Two young Americans, driving on the opposite side of the narrow roads searching for a soft-serve ice cream cone. Our laughter and screaming every inch of the trek bonded our friendship and left us with shots of joy as we traveled back to our homeland. (We returned the Land Rover without a scratch, by the way.)

55 // UNDER PRESSURE

The pressure of a number one ranking is indescribable. Somehow, I, a small-town girl from Northern Idaho, was ranked as the top female collegiate golfer by *Golf World* magazine.

It wasn't that I didn't deserve it; I had won nine college tournaments during my first three and a half years at San Jose State. But now, with my last semester of college ahead, I felt more pressure every single day than I ever had before. We were defending NCAA Champions, and I had yet to win the individual crown.

College golf is unique in that the main objective is to win as a team. But we also played as individuals against each other within the tournaments. It was about our team victories *and* how well we played independently. Expectations were high during those years, and I hated to let myself or anyone else down. I needed to work harder and play better at every event.

Now that my name was synonymous with high-level play, failure was not an option. Everyone was watching. At tournaments, I walked around the golf course smiling and joking, yet internally I was tightly wound, especially if I played mediocre rounds. My heart raced, my breath was shallow, my back hurt, and my body shook. *What if I played badly? What if I blew it? What if I wasn't really who people thought I was?*

Then I would rally for a victory and sigh with deep relief, taking my first full breath in hours. Fragile confidence drowned out the self-doubt … for a minute. I stood proudly on the podium and chose to enjoy the victory. Then I'd wake up the next morning and start all over again.

56 // A VICODIN-INDUCED FOG

I was about to turn the corner into my last semester in college. I had officially made it. Rumors were circulating that I was going to turn pro before graduating college, but my golf game wasn't ready and finishing school was important to me. I was going to be the first person in my family to graduate from a four-year college.

I shared the same apartment with the same people for the last year and a half, the female Campus Crusade staff member and a former collegiate field hockey player. We had a blast together. My boyfriend of over a year, Jeff, was planning to work in San Jose for the winter, which was good and bad. Our relationship had been rough lately and I had been noticing some odd behaviors. The winter was going to be a big test for us *and* for me. I hadn't been making good decisions in our relationship, a pattern that was all too familiar.

To make things more complicated, I was facing an impossible situation. To graduate, I needed two more classes I hadn't planned for in the spring semester. Attempting twenty-four credit hours in one spring semester along with golf practice and tournaments? Was it crazy? Yes. Was it possible? Maybe, just maybe. But I certainly would not be returning for an additional semester the following fall. I was so ready to leave California.

I skipped out of the junior writing workshop professor's office with my first victory. She agreed to let me complete the course on my own schedule, but the essay exams would be in her office. One down.

I fit the two concept and performance classes I needed—tennis and weightlifting—around golf practice. *Five classes left.*

There was a light at the end of the tunnel, albeit a murky one. I convinced my nutrition professor to let me miss Thursday classes if I borrowed notes from a friend. The other four classes could fall into place—if and only if the dean of the Human Performance Department (which covered physical education, adapted PE, exercise science, sports philosophy, and a couple more subjects) signed off.

I pleaded my case with eager confidence. The dean sat quietly for what seemed like an eternity. Finally, he turned his head in my direction. Since I had proven myself with a high GPA and was consistently on the Dean's List, he reluctantly signed off on my crazy plan. *Whew!* I gave a silent fist pump. As I headed home for the holidays, I felt invincible.

My breathing eased as I looked out over the familiar snow-covered golf course. I was happy to be home for a month on my last Christmas break. It felt surreal—there was only one more semester left of my collegiate career. I promised Coach Gale I wouldn't ski, but I didn't say anything about not playing basketball.

My basketball shoes were worn, but they still squeaked as I stepped onto the gym floor. The ball felt good in my hands, though my lungs heaved with effort after a couple runs up and down the court. I made up for my lack of height and strength with the guys by boxing out hard—really hard—and showing up scrappy.

Coach was there, as usual. We had had no intentional communication over the last couple years, just an occasional crossing of paths at the golf course or in the gym. Pick-up basketball felt like a safe space. The physical exertion of running up and down the court usually released the tension my body held.

I jumped as high as I could for a rebound, but was still far below the elbows of my competitors. I landed empty-handed. My attention shifted immediately from the lost ball to a funny feeling in my lower back—a *pop*, almost. I shook it off and ran a few more minutes before bowing out for the night.

Waking up the day after pick-up basketball usually came with some aches and pains. But this time my back throbbed more than normal. I iced it and popped some ibuprofen. It was fine. Of course it was fine.

Leaving home for my final semester felt bittersweet, but the California sun warmed me as I exited the San Jose Airport. Reality hit me full in the face: It was the first week of classes, and I had signed up to take 24 credit hours. *Who takes 24 credits?* I rushed through my morning classes, drove off to practice, and returned to campus for my evening class. It was going to be a long semester, and my carefully scheduled plans were about to be threatened.

After a week of practice, searing back pain attacked my body with a vengeance. I sat on the training table on the brink of tears. My athletic trainer, Heidi, was unable to hide her concern. "This is serious," she said.

I needed to see the school's orthopedic doctor for an MRI. The results delivered a blow: I had herniated the L4-L5 disc.

Heidi and the doctor stood stiffly in the examination room while Coach Gale paced back and forth. Chills of dread vibrated through my body as I listened to Coach bargaining with the doctor.

"She has to play. We need her to play," he stammered.

The doctor looked reluctant but said, "I don't think she can damage the nerve any more than she has, so it's up to her if she can handle the pain."

Three pairs of eyes stared down at me. "Of course I'm going to play," I said defiantly. "I'm not going to miss my last college season. And I'm not going to let my team down."

With a Vicodin prescription in hand, I resumed my normal chaotic schedule of events: class, treatment with Heidi, painkiller, practice, class, painkiller. *Repeat.*

I had trouble sitting for extended periods of time, so I had to find creative ways to get through class, like standing up in the back of the room. Coach Gale petitioned for me to use a pushcart in our tournaments. Through it all, I was in a Vicodin-induced fog.

Finally, it was May 1993. My nerves were frayed as I looked out over the University of Georgia's golf course ready for one more push: my final NCAA Championship. Even with a few injuries plaguing our team, we remained one of the favorites to win. A lot depended on that week. Mark Steinberg, a sports agent from IMG, (originally known as the International Management Group, an American global sports, events and talent management company) would be watching. Surgery loomed. I was not going to let myself, or my team, down. "I'll make myself get through this," I thought determinedly.

I had finished my last final exam the night before, proctored by Heidi at the hotel. I did it! I survived twenty-four credits and nine final exams. Wrapped in a back brace and the humiliation of having to use a pushcart on the course, I forced myself to prepare for my last championship as a collegiate athlete.

After three mediocre rounds, I was fourteenth entering my last collegiate round, which moved like molasses. As we walked up to the sixteenth tee box, Heidi informed me that there was a thirty-to-forty-five-minute back-up on the course. I collapsed to the ground, my eyes pleading with her. *No. I can't take any more.* She instinctively started to stretch out my hamstrings, soothing me with words of encouragement. I felt myself weakening with every passing minute.

The Georgia coach approached us, her face full of concern. "How are you holding up?" she asked. Through blurry eyes, I looked up at her. The words tumbled out of my mouth untamed, as if they'd been sitting there all along.

"Just get me off of this f*cking golf course."

But I somehow finished the round. Every step came with staggering pain.

57 // POMP AND CIRCUMSTANCE

My college graduation ceremony was the same weekend as the NCAA Championship tournament located in Georgia. There was no question in my mind—I was going to skip graduation and play, pain and all. We had a title to defend.

Unfortunately, we walked off the last hole with a third-place finish. Yes, we gave up our title, but we also accomplished a rare feat. In four years, our team accumulated a complete set of NCAA trophies: fourth place, second place, first place, and now, third place. I placed ninth, which was quite the surprise since I had wanted to quit mid-round with every ounce of my being.

I sat dutifully (and painfully) in my white plastic chair for our media debriefing. The long table we sat behind created some distance between us (me, my teammates, and Coach Gale) and the reporters as they ran through their list of obligatory questions.

"How disappointed are you not to win?" *Ummm ... very.*

I could hardly form any cohesive thoughts because of the searing sciatica pain pulsating in my back and left leg. I tried to make eye-contact with Heidi, pleading to get me an ice bag.

I stood up to leave, and Heidi and Lawrence Fan, our sports information director, flanked me on both sides. What was happening? My brain was foggy—those painkillers were kicking in. All of a sudden, my parents, my boyfriend Jeff, Coach Gale, my teammates, and others gathered in front of the table.

Lawrence clicked play on a cassette player. *Pomp and Circumstance* filled the air. Between the pain and exhaustion, I still could not figure out what all these people were doing. Heidi slid a golf visor fitted with a graduation tassel taped on the right side onto my head.

A smile lit up my face. I finally figured out the surprise. Coach Gale, Lawrence, Heidi, the interim SJSU President J. Handel Evans, and the University of Georgia's Associate Athletic Director Claude Felton, all had orchestrated a personalized graduation ceremony just for me.

I was delighted, and slightly embarrassed. Being the center of attention and celebrated by others has never been easy for me. I don't like being in the limelight, which is strange for an elite athlete.

President Evans's voice boomed through the cassette player as if he was standing right in front of me. "Congratulations for four successful years at San Jose State as a student-athlete." Lawrence handed me a San Jose State graduation folder and President Evans instructed me to move my tassel to the left, declaring me an official graduate of SJSU. Cheers, applause, and hugs all around.

This hot day in Athens, Georgia, will remain one of my most cherished memories. Lawrence and Heidi gave me the gift of being seen, loved, and celebrated. Nearly twenty-five years later, Lawrence wrote, "You had the same sparkle in your eyes that day as I remember from meeting you the first time."

The moment was seared into my memory, but the short reprieve slipped away as the pain surged throughout my back.

58 // A QUICK TRIP

It wasn't an ideal time to travel.

My sister, Debbie, and I arrived midday in Dallas, tossed our bags in the hotel room, and went straight to the pool deck to bask in the warm Texas sun. Senior year was officially over, and I was desperate for a few moments of rest and relaxation. The next day I was going to be honored as the nation's premier scholar-athlete in women's college golf and receive the distinguished Marilynn Smith Award. I had really wanted to accept the award in person, but it came at a personal cost.

During the two weeks following the end of my senior year and the NCAA National Championship tournament, I moved out of my apartment in San Jose, drove home to Idaho with my mom, and was squeezing in this quick trip to Texas before having back surgery.

Hectic was my modus operandi throughout all four years of college. I managed a busy athletic schedule and heavy academic load, and still graduated in four years with a 3.7 grade point average. I was a four-time NCAA All-American and I earned first-team Academic All-American three times. I made the Dean's List six times. I was awarded two-time SJSU scholar athlete of the year and SJSU Human Performance department outstanding graduate. And I won eleven golf tournaments.

While lying in the sun next to my sister, my thoughts drifted over the past year. This was the first time in months that I'd had to slow down and reflect. What a year it had been. Yet, it hardly compared to what was coming next, the bright lights of a surgery room.

59 // MY JOB IS REHAB

"Everything will be okay."

Heidi's voice was reassuring. I was so grateful she had flown from San Jose to watch over the doctor during my surgery. Over the next few hours, my future was in his hands.

"Thank you for being here," I told her.

My pain was beyond tolerable, and I was more than ready for surgery, but that didn't alleviate my embarrassment. I came home from Dallas with a backside on fire from sunburn. Not only would the doctor see my bright red skin, but I was also going to have to lie on the burn for days.

But my bruised ego wasn't going to stand in the way of this surgery. It was time. I counted backward and then … nothing.

I peeled my eyes open. Mom and Heidi looked back at me smiling. "It all went great, Tracy. The doctor is really pleased." My body felt heavy, and my words slurred. I drifted in and out a few more times before the nurses wheeled me to a room.

Unlike the doctor, I was certain that a one-night stay would be sufficient. Turns out, I was right. I escaped the confines of the hospital in less than thirty hours. Unfortunately, that was only step one of my recovery. I still had four weeks of lying flat on my back in bed. Mom converted one of our living rooms into a makeshift bedroom so I didn't have to tackle the stairs. The tradeoff was the total lack of privacy. Just thinking of it all made me tense and rigid.

Thank goodness I was able to start physical therapy after two weeks. Fourteen consecutive days of lying in bed was enough to make a person go insane. I was tired of watching endless hours of television, so Mom gave me a few novels to try out.

I actually hated reading despite being a good student. I learned to read what I needed to for class, but I never read a book for fun. I was willing to try anything at this point, though. Before I knew it, I was hooked. Who knew reading was fun? All it took was major back surgery for me to discover a new interest.

For the next eight weeks, rehab was my job. The physical therapist started me off with light movement and stretching. I pushed for more because more was always better, right? It's actually not.

"If you push too hard too fast you might never play golf again," was always the response. I obeyed the best I could. Doctors gave me the green light to swim on the days I didn't have therapy. It wasn't my favorite activity—I swam laps slowly and clumsily—but I was committed to accelerating the healing process and getting those clubs back into my hands. Amazingly, my back pain almost disappeared right after surgery, which made therapy a lot easier. Sometimes out of the blue, a twinge of pain would surge out of my back dropping me to my knees.

Six weeks post-op, the doctor gave me permission to swing my driver and hit a ball off the tee. I had been chipping and putting here and there, but I hadn't yet taken a swing. I was nervous, rightfully so. But I needed to start practicing if I was going to play in the upcoming LPGA Qualifying School (Q-School).

Mark Steinberg, the IMG sports agent who had watched me during the NCAA Championships, had gone on to recruit me. IMG was the largest sports agency in the world, and I was now a client. By simply signing the Q-School contract, I became a professional athlete.

Mark was very encouraging while I rehabbed, but I could tell he was antsy to hear how I was progressing. On paper I might be labeled a professional golfer, but it meant nothing until I played my way through Q-school and earned a spot on the LPGA Tour.

Now, gingerly, I bent over to rest the ball on the tee. I wiggled the club back and forth, a familiar feeling and weight that teased my hands. My heart raced and my breathing quickened. One more glance down the practice range. I moved the club back and through with about eighty-percent effort. As I watched the ball sail forward, I did a quick scan of my body and finally exhaled feeling very little pain.

With a grin spreading wide across my face, I had the long-awaited, hard-fought realization: *I'm back.*

60 // TWO DIFFERENT PEOPLE

Relationships are hard. Hurt and disappointment had left me wondering why I even tried in the first place. One relationship, during my sophomore year of college, hit me with the whirlwind sensation of infatuation—an emotional, all-consuming tidal wave that consumed reason, leaving me feeling dreamy, and tongue-tied. The push and pull of passion, overlaid with a lack of emotional maturity, broke the relationship and left me heartbroken in its wake.

The summer after my sophomore year I met Jeff while working at the TLV golf course. At first, I wasn't interested in his pursuits to date due to the recent heartbreak, but my heart eventually softened, and I said "yes" shortly before I was to leave for my third year of college.

A long-distance relationship before cell phones and email was not easy. Phone calls were expensive and handwritten letters a chore. Jeff traveled to a couple college tournaments during the fall and winter, but otherwise we spent most of our time together during my summer breaks. When I was home, our relationship flowed between playing golf, working together, and date nights. He was attentive and sweet. But when time and distance separated us, I experienced a different side of him.

I didn't want to believe the rumors about his drinking, but when he berated me with verbal assaults over the phone on several occasions, I started to believe it. *Was I dating two different people?*

When we first started dating, I did not want sex and constantly said "no." I didn't want to repeat what happened with Coach. I was also trying to follow God and what I had been learning about sexual purity through the CRU discipleship materials: sex outside of marriage is a sin so don't do it.

I tried to believe God forgave me for what happened with Coach. But the shame and negative beliefs that I was damaged, broken, and dirty still controlled how I felt in a relationship. Pieces of debris from the secret relationship with Coach left me closed off, disconnected from my own heart, and hypervigilant.

Early in our relationship, Jeff started asking me questions about my past and pressing me as to whether I had been hurt before. Flustered and feeling like I was disappointing him, I told Jeff about Coach. I said I didn't want the same kind of secret sexual relationship with him. Instead of feeling better, I felt worse.

Eventually I surrendered to Jeff's pressure. I didn't know how to connect with him emotionally, so I went to what worked before, being physically intimate as a way of connecting. But my spirit started to wither. I knew our relationship wasn't matching the teachings my Christian friends at college were committed to, and I was caught in trying to keep it a secret, again. I felt stuck in a web of ambivalence and numbness.

Jeff and I hadn't had much time together during the week he was with me and my family at my final NCAA Championship, or the gap between NCAAs and before my back surgery. My patience decreased with him over the last couple months of finishing my academic semester and playing my last college tournaments in a great deal of pain. I considered breaking up with him before going to Georgia, but I didn't have the capacity to add that to my plate.

When Jeff walked into my hospital room after back surgery, my frustration oozed out of me. "Just go home," I said curtly. My intensity surprised us both. "I want to be alone." After two years of push and pull, I was done.

Living in the same small community made it complicated. We both had to field people's questions, both spoken and unspoken. I was not prepared for his anger or how he turned on me. He accused me of not being a real Christian and blamed me for the broken relationship.

My anger pushed away my own emotional pain but the feeling that I was the problem that caused another relationship failure fed the shame already harboring in my soul.

Proud to be a freshman student-athlete on the SJSU Women's Golf team, fall 1989.

The formidable Coach Mark Gale, a retired Air Force colonel who led the SJSU Women's Golf program to three NCAA Division I championships during 19 seasons.

The biggest day of my career so far was at the 1991 U.S. Women's Public Links in Charlottesville, Va., where I won my first national amateur championship.

We were 1992 NCAA Women's Golf Champions, bringing home from Arizona State University's Karsten Golf Course at Tempe, Ariz., a third title for SJSU.

It was a high honor to represent the United States at the 1992 Curtis Cup -- the most prestigious team trophy for women amateur golfers from the U.S., Great Britain, and Ireland.

Our last NCAA tournament was the same weekend as my graduation. Coach Gale (left), sports info director Lawrence Fan, and others surprised me with a private ceremony, complete with "Pomp and Circumstance" on a cassette and a tassel on my sun visor.

PART FOUR:
THE AFTER

61 // Q-SCHOOL TAKE ONE

Why pay a lot of money to go back to school only a few months after graduating from college? I had been asked the question more times than I could count.

"No, LPGA Qualifying School is not what it sounds like," I would explain to the people in my life who knew nothing about golf. I can't really blame them. Golf has a reputation for being complicated, and "Q-School" only makes it more baffling.

"It's not going back to school. It's a series of golf tournaments to qualify for the LPGA Tour."

Tour Qualifying School dates to 1965. It still is used today as a series of tournaments an aspiring golfer must survive in order to qualify to play on the LPGA Tour. When I entered the LPGA tour qualifying process, there were three stages by which to earn this coveted exemption known as your "tour card": first, second, and final stage. Under the LPGA regulations in 1993, a player went straight to the Final Stage if she made it through the First Stage cut. The cut was based strictly off of score. If a player didn't make the First Stage cut, then she would try again at Stage Two. A player also might take a chance and bypass Stage One, choosing to only play Stage Two, but it was not advised.

At the Final Stage, the top twenty-five players based on score earned an exempt tour card, which gave them the right to play in any LPGA event except majors, which had specific qualifications. The next twenty-seven received non-exempt status, which made them able to play in LPGA events based on field size and strength.

My doctors gave me the green light two months after my back surgery to enter both the First Stage and Second Stage tournaments. When I signed the application and paid my entry fee, I became a professional golfer.

The First Stage was played in Venice, Florida. My back wasn't at full strength, but I wanted, needed, to try. It was the first time I played a full week of golf since the NCAAs a couple months prior. I missed the cut for the top thirty by two shots.

Disappointed, I regrouped and prepared for the Second Stage tournament to be played under the one-hundred-degree desert sun in Rancho Mirage, California. If I didn't make it through this stage, my once-in-a-year (which felt more like a once-in-a-lifetime) opportunity to play on the LPGA Tour would disappear.

My family, North Idaho community, peers, and IMG were all waiting and watching with much anticipation. Could I make the transition from college golf star to the LPGA Tour? The hope-filled expectations were tangible. My own expectations were even higher but slightly less hopeful. *Could I really do it?*

Mom jumped at the opportunity to come with me to Rancho Mirage, California, for Stage Two. We nestled into the Holiday Inn & Suites and I was grateful to not have to spend the week alone. The pressure to make it through the next three rounds felt more oppressive than the heat.

After a solid first two rounds, I had the lead at one-over par. I had some breathing room, but I knew it's never over until the last putt drops. My nerves surged at the start of my third round and I got off to a rough start. Doubt crept in and I swung the club tentatively. The back nine didn't get any easier as the club felt heavy and foreign in my hands.

That's the frustrating thing about golf. No matter how much you practice and play, sometimes it's just not your day. I finished with a seventy-eight. The good news was that even with that score, I remained in the top thirty.

I was moving on to the Final Stage. I was overcome with mixed emotions. One part of me was thrilled to be advancing to Daytona Beach. Another part was overwhelmed with the amount of physical and mental work ahead over the next month. My back was getting stronger, but my golf stamina over multiple days needed to expand.

There was no room in the Final Stage of Q-School for anything less than perfection. Only three and a half months post back surgery, I wasn't sure if my mental and physical endurance were up to the challenge. And if Stage Two was any indication, the level of skill the Final Stage of Q-School demanded was going to be unlike any competition I had faced before.

More than the Curtis Cup. More than the NCAA golf championship. More than the high school state basketball finals.

This was my chance to make history, to be an LPGA Tour Professional for the forty-fourth season of the LPGA Tour (1994). It was now or never, or so it felt. But that wasn't exactly the case. I could try again the following year.

Mom and I flew to Daytona Beach together. Her presence was such a gift again, and it seemed like our relationship was getting closer.

The course at Indigo Lakes Golf Course was an old-style, tree-lined course with stringy Bermuda grass. After playing the majority of my golf in the north and the west, I didn't have a clue about how to chip or putt on Bermuda grass. It's not smooth and consistent like bentgrass in the Northwest. I hired a tour caddy for the tournament, a recommendation from my former assistant coach at SJSU. Tour caddies are men and women who travel with the LPGA Tour on a regular basis. Having a veteran caddy by my side for the week felt reassuring. I knew I was going to need to rely on him to help me navigate this course.

I recognized some of my competitors from college golf. The unfamiliar faces were current tour players attempting to improve or re-earn their tour card from the previous season. At this moment, all my college golf success felt like a distant memory. I was no longer a big fish in a small pond.

My first two rounds, seventy-six and seventy-nine, were defensive and tentative … again. I couldn't shake my anxious nerves, especially on the greens. I missed so many makeable putts. My back was tired, but the pain remained nominal. Mom watched every shot, every putt, making sure I stayed hydrated and nourished. Her presence grounded me from totally losing it.

I dialed in on my third round with an even par of seventy-two, and I just made the cut to play the final round. There was no television coverage at Q-school and hardly any gallery of onlookers, but the pressure was palpable with so much at stake.

My body and mind were tired after five days of golf. As I prepared for my final day of play, my back pain was noticeable, although nothing compared to what it was like before surgery.

Entering round four, one of the non-exempt tour cards was still attainable—until the wheels came off. I lost my confidence, my feel, and all my positive energy. I let my mind beat me. Negative words spewed from my mouth, and I became paralyzed with fear.

Gazing at the scoreboard, tears trickled down my face. I missed the top fifty-two by four shots. I didn't make it. I disappointed my agent Mark, my parents, and my sponsors.

What am I going to do now?
Where will I play next year?
Am I really good enough to do this?
Am I fooling myself?

62 // A NEW PLAN

I twirled my club and took two breaths.

I can do this. I can do this.

Just a few holes earlier, I wanted to give up. The leaderboard following us around mocked me. On display for all to see: *Tracy Hanson falls four strokes behind. Sorry for your loss. Better luck next time.*

Here I am in a foreign country. I didn't even know where Indonesia was before traveling to Southeast Asia to play the Ladies Asian Tour. The disappointment of not making the LPGA Tour still stung a year later. Now, the possibility of another big letdown at the Ladies Indonesian Open, the third of four professional tournaments on the schedule. My resolve heightened; I had not come all this way to finish four strokes behind.

I can do this. I can do this.

I dropped a birdie putt on hole 14 and told myself the lead is still within reach. Call it grit. Call it my competitive spirit. Whatever it was, my momentum shifted. The outside world disappeared, and my focus narrowed. I went into attack mode. Another birdie and an eagle on a par 5 carried me to the end of the round. I fought back to a tie for first and was quickly whisked away for a playoff.

After tentatively pushing my drive into the right rough on the first playoff hole, I launched my ball toward the green like an arrow in search of a bullseye. The sun's glare invaded my sightline. I couldn't see where it landed but I knew it must be good because I heard the screams and saw my friends jumping.

My gait quickened toward the green. We don't run in golf. But I wouldn't have put it past me at that moment. After the longest walk of my golf life, my non-English-speaking caddy and I made it to the green and saw it for ourselves. My ball was resting two inches away from the hole. My knees went weak. I tapped in my birdie putt and waited, holding back tears and a smile. I was minutes away from winning my first professional golf tournament.

Traveling to Asia hadn't been on the top of my list after my failure at

Qualifying School in 1993. But I didn't really have another option. Thankfully, IMG had a worldwide network in place and was instrumental in helping me put together a contingency plan. My first year as a professional golfer started half-way around the world with the Ladies Asian Tour, a four-week swing with 120 female golf professionals who competed from Thailand to Malaysia to Indonesia to Taiwan.

The tour organizers paid out the prize money in cash, and after a second place, a win, and two top 15th place finishes in Thailand and Taiwan, my fanny pack was bulging with my winnings. I was so ready to go home with my Order of Merit award (top money list winner on the tour) and roughly $25,000 in total.

The Asian Tour provided a great experience to kickstart my first professional year. Now I was on to the rest of an action-packed schedule. IMG worked its magic to secure me sponsor invites to four Ladies European events later in the summer, and even an opportunity to play in my second LPGA Tour event in Boston in the fall. By the time the season was over, I had traveled to thirteen countries in twelve months, all with one goal in mind: making the 1995 LPGA Tour.

I can do this.

63 // Q-SCHOOL TAKE TWO

The distant thunder and dark clouds on the horizon seemed fitting for the occasion. It's one of those moments where the outside weather matched what was happening to me on the inside. I felt grumbly, unpredictable, and irritated staring down the fairway of the fifteenth hole (my first nine) during the first round of the Final Stage of LPGA Q-School. The pressure felt heavy, and I'm not just talking about the barometric pressure.

An entire year has passed since not making the 1994 Final Q-School cut. After twelve months and a lot of travel, I found myself in familiar, albeit somewhat terrifying, territory: Q-School Final Stage "take two." The last thing I needed was a rain delay on my first round.

The thunder rumbled as I watched my second shot fall short into the right greenside bunker. Not again.

What are you doing, Tracy?

You suck, Tracy.

My inner critic jumped right in as usual.

I grabbed my sand wedge from the bag and slid down into the sand trap just as the airhorn signaling a rain delay echoed throughout the golf course. As soon as the horn blew, we were required to stop playing. I couldn't hurry and take my shot. Now I not only had a terrible shot, but I was going to have wet sand to contend with. *Great. Just great.* My caddy and good friend, Loopy (her real name was Maria), and I headed back to the clubhouse to wait out the storm with the other hundred-plus players and caddies.

Once the weather cleared, the horn blew twice signaling the restart. I had been taking practice swings with my sand wedge to stay loose. Now it was go-time. I inhaled a deep breath and exhaled slowly as I stepped down into the bunker. I raised up on my tippy toes to glance at the downslope where I needed to land the ball. Then I nestled into my bull-legged stance. *Breathe. Rhythm. Relax.*

I tightened my hands around my grip and put my swing in motion. The splash of sand sent my ball up and out. I watched and waited to see how far it would roll off the sharp left to right slope. As long as it wasn't too far, I'd be okay.

I jumped out of the bunker just in time to see the ball disappear into the cup. A birdie! Instinctively, my arms shot upward and I found Loopy's eyes. Adrenaline flooded my body and the momentum from that shot energized my attitude.

I can do this. It never ceases to amaze me how quickly the tide—my attitude—can turn, hot and cold, up and down, good and bad.

We played until darkness stopped play. I was playing well, but would have to keep the positive energy going when we restarted early in the morning. I did. I played twenty-five holes to complete round one and two. The momentum rolled into the third and fourth rounds too.

With my emotions caught in my throat, I stared at the leaderboard that told a much different story from my second LPGA Tour Final Stage in the Fall of 1994. My name was written in the 5-under heading and added up to a twelfth-place finish.

I thought back to that bunker birdie shot on day one. It was a pivotal moment in helping me to four rounds of seventy-two, seventy-one, sixty-nine, and seventy-one. Tears of joy and relief filled my eyes. I just earned my 1995 LPGA Tour Rookie card.

I did it.

64 // ROOKIE OF THE YEAR … ALMOST

I began to calculate if I could make my flight as I walked down the eighteenth fairway. While I signed my scorecard, Kenny could start packing my golf clubs in the travel bag. I would have to dash to the locker room and grab my luggage and miscellaneous junk. Hopefully, the transportation vehicle would be waiting as I'd asked.

The battle for *Rookie of the Year* was tight. I was neck-and-neck with Pat Hurst, one of my former teammates at San Jose State. Points were awarded based on where a player finished in each tournament throughout 1995. Pat was playing in the group in front of me, finishing her final round of the 1995 regular season.

"Focus, Tracy. You need to make birdie." My bogey on hole seventeen might be my demise.

My rookie year on the LPGA Tour had been eye-opening. To play with the best female golfers in the world, tenacity and perseverance are required. The reality: I learned that a handful of great weeks could add up to a successful year, even if the other weeks were average or mediocre. But the worst results, by far, was missing a cut.

Each week, back when I played and still today, 144 golfers start play for most LPGA tournaments. Some weeks the number changes due to available daylight hours. After the completion of the first two rounds, the low seventy players by score and ties make the cut to play the weekend. I only earned a paycheck if I made the cut and played on Saturday and Sunday.

I also learned during my first season on tour that when I missed the cut, as I did many times, all I wanted to do was hightail it out of town. Unfortunately this wasn't an option on most weekends. Changing travel plans is costly—money I didn't make by missing the cut. Instead, I tried to remove the sting of failure by practicing or finding something away from the course to explore.

Traveling from one city to the next, week after week, wasn't too bad. Staying mentally sharp and keeping up with life and relationships outside of golf, however, was exhausting. Loopy caddied for me the first six tournaments of the season; I was grateful for a familiar face around. I didn't have to worry about juggling caddies on top of everything else, and I was able to get settled and comfortable in tour life.

The week came, though, when I had to hire a tour caddy. Two great candidates were available, and it split me in two. I wanted to hire them both, but I had to make a business decision—which person would be able to help me most? Saying "yes" to one meant disappointing the other. I finally chose Kenny, who had caddied for me during the weekend rounds at my first Women's British Open in 1994. And he was the one with me on my last hole of my LPGA rookie season.

Four tournaments in a row felt ideal, but I did end up playing six back-to-back on two different stretches. When I did take a week off, it was busy and not overly restful. Between family, friends, and a man I started dating, I was being pulled to opposite corners of the States. No matter which priority I chose, I always seemed to disappoint someone on the other side.

After my fourth-place finish in St. Louis the week before this final tournament, I was close behind Pat Hurst in the Rookie of the Year race. At the beginning of this week, I traveled to Charlotte, North Carolina, but my clubs enjoyed a trip to Tampa. On top of practicing without my clubs, the first hotel I stayed in was *disgusting*. I barely made it through one night. On Wednesday, I checked into a new place. It was a harsh start to the week.

I evaluated my downhill lie over water. My heart raced and adrenaline pulsed through my veins. I caught it clean and watched it rocket toward the pin. I tapped in for a par. It's going to be close.

I sprinted off the green—I still didn't know who captured Rookie of the Year as the final numbers still needed to be tallied. I saw the transportation car waiting to rush me to the airport. I focused on signing my card, and, as I exited the scorer's tent, a reporter wanted to talk to me. "Real quick," I said, thinking only of my flight. "I have a plane to catch."

I made it to the airport with just enough time to walk onto my flight back to Idaho. I had played a solid week of golf—probably my best all-around ball striking of the year with rounds of sixty-nine, seventy-two, seventy-one, and sixty-nine. My dumb bogeys held me to an eleventh-place finish. I got in my own way a bit, but I also played more relaxed than I usually do. It was out of my control now.

The contest came down to the last round of the last eligible tournament. Pat finished two shots better than me in the final standings of the tournament and I lost Rookie of the Year by five points. One shot made the difference.

Golf truly is a game of inches.

65 // FELLOWSHIP

The notice on the information board announced that Fellowship would be held late afternoon on Tuesday. The timing felt perfect: I could play my practice round, get my after-play practice on the range and putting green done, and still grab a short workout in the fitness van—the LPGA's traveling semi-truck that expanded to serve as our physical therapy and fitness room.

The familiar faces of my LPGA Tour friends greeted me as I entered the meeting room. With a deep sigh, I dropped into a seat. It had been a *long* day, and the weekly Christian Fellowship meeting available for players, caddies, and staff was one hour where I experienced rest from the demands of tour life. Fellowship served as our "church."

I walked into life on the LPGA Tour with the same Christian faith I had developed in college. I believed in God and wanted to follow Jesus, but I still felt the push-and-pull of *being on* for Jesus. The not-so-subtle message for Christian professional athletes can be to use our platform to share the gospel. In other words, *rah-rah Jesus*. (I can hear my own cynicism, which I'll set aside for a moment.)

As a professional athlete, I have always accepted that I have a responsibility to be a role model. However, it's too easy for the Christian community to assume Christian professional athletes are perfect human beings. There's an expectation that we will always point upward when we achieve something, and never show frustration, pain, or anger in failing. That is unkind and unrealistic. Jesus is the lighthouse of my orientation, but there sure are a lot of foggy days.

I scanned over my journal entry, satisfied with what I'd written.

> *Lord, grant me a spirit of wisdom and revelation in the deep knowledge of yourself. Flood the eyes of my heart with light so that I can know and understand the hope to which you have called me. Make known to me your glorious inheritance. Lord, allow me to know and understand the immeasurable and unlimited and surpassing greatness of your power for me that is demonstrated in the worship of your mighty strength.*

Referencing scriptures like Colossians 1:9–12 by putting pen to paper helped me center my thoughts on God. I didn't always feel like what I wrote in my journal was *true*, but I would keep trying. I still do.

As I flipped a few pages back, I noticed that my prayers slanted toward asking for results. I wonder what God thinks of these prayers. *Are they selfish? Does He actually care about helping me succeed?* Here's an example:

Lord, I ask that you supernaturally play through me this week. Holy Spirit, take control of the results and enable me to give my best—one shot at a time. I ask that you bless me with a win. Amen.

I wanted to believe that God cared about the smallest details of my life, but I wasn't wholly convinced. Or, maybe, I just didn't completely trust Him yet.

Connecting with other Christian players at Fellowship offered a moment to consider my silent questions while I sifted through the weeds of hardship on tour. The LPGA Tour didn't run the Fellowship, but our chaplain, Cris Stevens, was supported by the tour and she was considered a part of the LPGA Tour family. As LPGA players and competitors, we didn't share on a deep level, but we at least could connect on a spiritual level and share our golf struggles.

We finally settled on a day and time for our small group to meet. You'd think that getting six players together who are at the same golf course every day would be easy. *Oh no.* Some weeks, four days would pass before I saw one of my friends on the weekend. Our small group gave us the opportunity for deeper Bible study and a little more vulnerability.

As competitors, we had to keep up some semblance of a guard with one another. I wore my mask well. Performing for Jesus became an extension of my golf performance, hoping it would sooth my ingrained negative belief that I'm only as good as my performance. *Hide the pain; play for an audience of one.*

I have much gratitude for my Christian friends on Tour and how the Fellowship provided space in those years from 1995 to 2009 to gather together during our competitive days. As I have reflected on my own dilemma with performance expectations throughout my golf career, I have come to realize playing for an audience of one, Jesus, is another way of staying stuck in results-oriented pursuits.

Performing for Jesus only perpetuated my performance-based acceptance and identity. If Jesus lives in me, then He can't be in the crowd watching. Instead, He is doing it *with* me. Something I am still learning.

66 // AFTER-HOURS ADVENTURES

I tugged. The hook sank deeper. *Ugh, not again.* Squatty trees littered the reservoir. "Pull gently while keeping the pole straight," came a voice behind me. In between rescuing our lures, we caught nearly thirty fish in total. As invited guests by a local sponsor for the Corning Classic, we were given two rules: Catch and release, and have fun.

My finesse with a forty-yard pitch shot far surpassed my ability to cast a lure on target. On our second outing to the reservoir, I snagged a tree root lurking beneath the water. I pulled and pulled. I heard a *snap* as the tension of the pole gave way. I stumbled back and then froze, realizing my rod hadn't survived the root.

"I'm pretty sure I'm getting the *look* behind me," I said. *Oops—my aggression had won again.* "I'm sorry, Loopy," I apologized, "I'll buy you a new one."

Loopy's sister, Nancy, and I spun into uncontrollable laughter, culminating in tears and belly cramps.

Many of the tour stops had good fishing in the golf course ponds. I enjoyed fishing for small and big mouth bass. I needed my own rod and bait, so I went on a shopping spree and bought new gear to travel with when I had my car on the road.

As instructed, I pointed my new rod toward the water and gently twitched the tip. My new top-water lure jumped in my direction slightly and emitted a subtle *bloop*. The pond, which ran along number nine, glimmered in the Tennessee dusk. A gentle breeze cooled our skin after a long, hot day of golf.

I listened, watched, and waited. A top-water fisherwoman must always be ready. *Bam!* A large-mouth bass exploded out of the water with my lure in its mouth. A split-second later, the fight was on. Adrenaline rushed through my body. I got into position, feet shoulder-width apart and knees flexed. I pulled the pole upward to keep the line tight. The fish thrashed and the drag whistled as the line went with it. Tug-of-war ensued. *Reel in, hold firm. Reel in, hold firm.*

The fish tired before I did. I grabbed the struggling bass by its lower lip.

After extricating the hook, I said *thank you*, leaned in for a pretend kiss, and gently placed it back in the water. For a few moments, fishing the golf course ponds was a welcome reprieve from the insistent golf thoughts that flooded my mind.

Another mid-summer adventure came at the Canadian Open with the Rocky Mountains looming in the distance.

"Let's go to the Canada Olympic Park and do the luge run!" somebody said. We piled into the rental car for the thirty-five-minute drive to northwest Calgary.

Giddy, and a bit nervous about this spontaneous adventure, I surveyed the landscape. Ski jumps and tube-like paths littered the hillside.

I watched my friend disappear around the first corner. I was scared, but my love for speed fastened my helmet and I cozied onto the sled. We were going down the luge feet-first—unlike the Olympic lugers, who go head-first. We weren't on the steepest part of the track, but it still was real, solid ice with dangerous potential.

Relax, I was told, and the sled would glide. Easier said than done—my career teetered on the edge of disaster with one wrong move. My shoulders felt like lead, rigid with tension through the first few turns. Laid out in a prone position, I peeked over my boots and became one with the luge

"That was awesome!" I screamed as the sled came to a stop.

As seasons passed along, the fishing and exploring local sights were replaced with longer practice sessions, more workouts, added sponsor obligations. This depleted any extra time at the end of the day.

I still tried to hang out with friends who were involved with our Christian Fellowship. Sharing similar values, beliefs, and interests provided a grounding rod amidst the chaos of travel and grind of performance. There were a few with whom I shared hotel rooms and host families. These women became some of my closest friends on tour.

But, again, vulnerability had limits when friendship and competition converged. Sharing our golf performance struggles flowed easily enough. Speaking of our heartaches, wounds, or life challenges, however? Not so much.

67 // GRIMY HOTELS AND PRIVATE HOUSING

I paid for everything on tour: my flights, lodging, food … even my caddy.

People often seem surprised to hear that life as a professional golfer is not as glamorous as it may appear. My annual costs during these years ranged from $50,000 to $70,000 per year to play on the LPGA Tour. Sometimes after making the cut and finishing near the bottom of the list, I still walked away in the red.

I was thankful for the few endorsements (companies who pay me to wear their logo) that helped offset my spending, but I still felt the pressure to pinch dollars whenever I could. I had a mortgage on my Florida condo, utilities, health and disability insurance, car maintenance, and other general living expenses to keep up with just like most people.

I scoured the hotel market near our tournament course in New Jersey, discouraged. Everything was *so* expensive. I settled on a Best Western about ten minutes away. When I walked in, my revulsion matched the look on Lori's face. She was my roommate for the week. The further I ventured into the dingy hotel room, the more I could feel the dirt crawling up my skin.

"This is gross," I said.

Lori had already been checking out other options. We had to sleep here tonight. But the next day, we hightailed it out of that hell hole.

As an introvert, there were only a few players I enjoyed rooming with. Lori was one of them. If she or a few others weren't available, I splurged and stayed by myself, which was a nice treat.

Private housing, offered at each LPGA tournament for any player interested in staying with a local family, was a wonderful option to save on hotel expenses. It also could play another important role: it soothed the ache of loneliness while on the road. My first couple years on tour, I garnered some amazing host families that I continued to return to, and many I still keep in touch with today. My ratio between hotels and private housing was roughly 50–50 over the course of a typical season.

I had one really bad private housing situation. Since the hotels in the New York suburbs are pricey, I put in a request for me and Loopy, who was caddying for me. We arrived at the host family's house in the late afternoon. The woman of the house welcomed us warmly and showed us around. "We would love to take you to our club for dinner," she told us. We agreed and settled into our rooms.

That pleasant first night disintegrated into open negativity from the wife and emotional outbursts from the husband. By day three I was ready to pull out my hair. "Loopy, we are moving out," I declared. "I'll find us a hotel." Sometimes, saving money wasn't worth the turmoil. It was the first (and only) time I left private housing.

Most of the families I stayed with year after year became like extended family. Decades later, I still stay in touch with and visit some of my "road families" all over the United States. Walking through their doors always feels a bit like coming home Private housing with people like this was truly a gift.

68 // SIXTY-THREE: A CAREER BEST

"Kenny, did you see our tee time?"

An ominous tightness moved through my chest, matching the June sky above. It wasn't the first time I had been paired with Annika for the first two rounds, and it wouldn't be the last. It was 1996 and the week before she had won her second U.S. Women's Open. She had become a *big deal.*

Play. Stop. Play. Stop. Rhythm wandered off with each blare of the airhorn. Rain delays tired me, both physically and emotionally. And my back didn't do well under those conditions. While focusing on my own play, which included a first-round sixty-eight, I kept an eye on Annika. She was a machine. Her hypnotic rhythm never changed.

I was in the middle of the pack after the first two rounds of the Oldsmobile Classic being played in East Lansing, Michigan, and seven shots back from the leaders, but I would be playing on the weekend. *Anything can happen.* The course was soft, and the skies had cleared.

My first two holes were innocent pars, but something felt *different.* Then, it started. Hole three: five-iron within four feet—birdie. Six-iron on number four to a foot and a half—birdie. Half sand wedge left me a fourfoot birdie putt on number five.

I felt comfortable. I felt a rhythm. I had entered *the zone.*

Another five iron to four feet on number nine: my fourth birdie.

While Kenny double-checked my alignment and chatted casually with me about movies and sports, the birdies kept dropping.

My six-iron conquered hole ten with a three-foot birdie putt. Eight-iron to six feet on number eleven. My trusty wedge to nine feet on twelve dropped in birdie number seven. The long, par-three thirteenth hole required my four-iron, and I cozied it right up to ten feet. *Five holes, five birdies.* A total of eight for the round.

Wide-eyed at the super-sized gallery who had appeared out of nowhere, I looked over at Kenny. His unwavering gaze said, "I've got you." My name was on the leaderboard and my heart was skipping with excitement.

I came out of my trance and nervously parred the next four holes.

Kenny and I stood together on the eighteenth tee looking down the slight uphill par-four. A ballooning crowd filled the fairway and greenside grandstands. One more birdie and I would shoot my personal best.

My legs were shaking as I peered over my putt on the eighteenth green. The crowd was eerily quiet. At the clink of the ball at the bottom of the cup, the crowd erupted. I made my ninth birdie and carded my personal best—a 63!

69 // THIS TIME?

Just when I felt hopeless at making a romantic relationship work, I was sideswiped by a secret crush from college. Back then, every time I caught a glimpse of Ron in class or spotted him walking toward me in the hallway, my heart would skip a beat. We joked around like siblings with side hugs, and it stopped there. After all, he was dating a girl who looked like a model. I *knew* he wouldn't be interested in anything more than a platonic friendship with me. Or so I thought.

Out of the blue, Ron reached out and said he wanted to come watch me play at the LPGA tournament in Sacramento. I was stunned. When I heard his laughter and spotted his smile in the gallery during my round, butterflies fluttered in my stomach, and I stumbled a bit. There is no denying that I still had feelings for him. Apparently they were reciprocated.

One date ignited passionate sparks between us. A relationship wouldn't be easy—I lived at this point in Florida, he lived in California—but we had to give it a shot. Back to long-distance, letters, and calling cards, coupled with lengthy plane rides. (This was all before cell phones.) Unlike my previous long-distance relationships during college, I felt hopeful this time was going to be different. This was everything I wanted. Yet, I still felt so scared.

Within a few months, he said he loved me. Things were moving fast in those months in 1996 and 1997. Passion burned, boundaries blurred, and guilt and confusion weighed heavy on my shoulders. I was afraid of committing to a relationship and I wanted a relationship with this man at the same time.

We started talking about marriage. *Do I love him? How will I know? Can I trust him? Can I trust myself?* My head was split in two directions. My uncertainty clouded my heart. I thought I loved him, but I was so scared that I was going to mess this relationship up like the others.

We had shared briefly about our past relationships, but I hadn't told Ron about my relationship with Coach yet. I had not recognized at this point in time that what happened was abuse. Instead, the unjustified guilt I felt made me fearful.

My mind swirled with questions. How can I tell the man I think I want to marry that I had a secret relationship with my coach who was married? *Will he be disgusted? Will he change his mind about me?*

70 // TRAVEL WARS

My long stretch of travel started eight weeks earlier after an already exhausting week of rain delays in Rochester, New York. I packed up and hopped a flight to Philadelphia for the next tournament in Atlantic City, New Jersey. I played well in the first two rounds and my name was on the leaderboard, but another rainy day soaked through my raingear and wrung my momentum dry. On top of being disappointed in my finish, thunderstorms left me stranded in the Philly airport.

When I stumbled exhausted into Toledo barely before the clock struck midnight, I begged for a pillow and some much-needed sleep. This was the reality of life on tour. One week turned into two, three, and then four. When one tournament ended, we packed up and did it all again in a new city. Some weeks allowed a rest day on Monday, but often I ended up playing an extra charity pro-am event (one pro paired with four amateurs as one team) to earn extra income. These events might be at the current tournament site, but more often than not, they were in a completely different city, adding more travel to the week.

There were some side benefits at certain LPGA Tour stops. Toledo, one of my favorite stops on the LPGA Tour, was full of fun extracurricular activities. One night, a local family hosted a party—great food and boats to hunt for fish in the super-sized pond behind their house. Our quest for who could catch the biggest bass entertained us until dark.

My dad had flown in for the tournament. He had not been to a tournament outside the western states since my senior year of college. I invited him to fish, but he declined.

It wasn't normal for Dad to come to a tournament by himself. Awkward space lingered between us most of the time. Honestly, I'm so thankful he had never tried to be my coach. Decades of unspoken desire for his love and adoration, however, bound my heart to him. The best way I knew how to connect was through my success. I didn't disappoint this week, shooting a sixty-four on Saturday. I felt aloof but focused. It was a rare round when I wasn't aware of my score until I added it up at the end.

I dropped Dad off at the Toledo airport on Sunday night. Loopy, who had come to hang out in Toledo, and I scooted over to Youngstown, Ohio, so that I could play a quick practice round on Monday for our next tournament. Then, I turned around and drove back to the Cleveland airport in time to drop her off at Departures and welcome Ron with a big hug at Arrivals.

I carved out two days to enjoy each other before heading back to Youngstown for the tournament. The orangutans amused us at the zoo, and we purchased a new rod for fishing the golf-course ponds. Ron flew back home to California, and I went on to have a solid finish on Sunday in Youngstown. Time for a welcomed two-week break from tournament play—but not travel.

I zoomed back to Cleveland and jumped on a plane for Spokane, Washington, Sunday evening. I hadn't been home in seven months. I missed my mountains and my mom. Ron flew in from California to attend a high school friend's wedding and planned to meet my parents for the first time. I felt nervous, but I knew they would like him.

The week flew by in the blink of an eye. Now it was my turn to head to California to spend my second week off with my guy's family and our friends from college. My two-week break didn't feel very restful with the constant bouncing around. A favorite part of the week with Ron and his parents was catching my first wild salmon in Monterey Bay in between Dramamine naps. When we cooked it up for dinner that night, fresh caught salmon catapulted to the top of my favorite meal list.

After another sad goodbye, I headed out on a three-week tour stretch to Edmonton, Canada; Boston; and then over "the pond" to England for the British Open. Mom and PāPā came to Edmonton to watch me play. Ron flew back to Boston for part of the week. And then, in England, I'd be all on my own. If it resembled anything like the year before, it would be a lonely week.

My feet started killing me in Canada. The physical therapist diagnosed the issue as plantar fasciitis. On a scale of one to ten, my feet throbbed at seven and my lower back hovered around four most days. When I arrived in Boston, the FootJoy shoe rep hooked me up with a biomechanics doctor. I vehemently hoped that the handmade orthotics would be the answer. Only time would tell.

The Boston Tournament went by so fast, I thought as the boarding door closed. The plane hadn't begun to move backwards yet when an odd sound reverberated through the cabin, lifting heads and drawing anxious looks. Several long minutes passed before the crackle of the speaker overhead garnered our attention.

"It appears that the plane next to us has just clipped our left wing and the wings are currently touching," the captain announced. "We have to wait for the FAA to come look at both planes before we can move. Unfortunately, no one can get out of their seats for fear of shifting the balance of the plane."

Groans filled the cabin.

One hour. Two hours. Three hours. Impatience mounted. Still, the FAA was nowhere in sight. It was late and I was hungry and tired.

At the five-hour mark, the captain shared the news that we were finally cleared to depart. *No damage to the wing.* I dozed off, dreaming about what transpired a few days prior, making my flight across "the pond" pass quickly enough.

Even at age twenty-five, I was still in shock that we were *really* going to do it; *we were going to get married.* Yes, Ron and I kind of spontaneously, and a bit unorthodoxly, got engaged while he was in Boston. We had a ring, but we had made a loose agreement to wait a while before he would officially propose. Ron's excitement, one of the qualities I enjoyed about him, was too much for him to bear and in the middle of a conversation about waiting, he convinced both of us, why not now? We walked out of the bedroom at my friend's house on an emotional high, announcing we were engaged.

Going off to opposite sides of the world after getting engaged popped my emotional high back to reality. I had a tournament to play, and communication back home was going to be sporadic at best. I needed to focus on my golf. Meanwhile, Ron went back to California and the comforts of home and family and friends.

Being alone in England fostered my doubts and fears. I had questions. So many questions. *Are we ready for this? Am I ready for this?* I still needed to focus on finishing the rest of my season strong and move up the money list. It all started to feel like a lot.

As I landed back stateside after an up-and-down week, I felt overwhelmed and exhausted. Two emotions that often led me to emotionally disconnect from others, including Ron. I did my best to push my doubts and questions to the back of my mind, but they were never too far away

71 // ALONE AGAIN

Our parents were not overly enthused about our engagement. My dad quickly shot down the idea. "Why do you want to get married?" he asked. "It'll ruin your career." His mom was mostly worried about life beyond the golf course. "What about when you have a baby?"

"We have childcare on tour, and I'll take the baby with me," I answered defensively. *I can do this.*

But, as the weeks and months passed, I began to question again if *this* is what I wanted. Ron and I had real issues to work through, and neither one of us were skilled at navigating difficult conversations well.

I told him about what happened in high school. His response made me freeze. His lack of compassion and anger on my behalf caused a piece of my heart to close off.

Like a slow oil leak, our relationship began to feel more burdensome than joyful. Anger, shame, and empty promises ate away at my hope that we could make this work.

Fifteen months after Ron came back into my life, I had to choose to let go. With a heavy heart I broke off our engagement. I instinctively stuffed my grief and covered the loss and my broken heart by focusing all my attention on the second half of the 1997 Tour schedule. I needed some good finishes to move up the money list (the main determiner of retaining exempt status on tour). I wanted no more distractions. But my inner critic was loud.

You're damaged goods. It's your fault you can't make relationships work, the voice of shame whispered over and over in my ear.

All the old voices started yammering away. *I'm the problem. I am terrible at love. My track record proves it. Will I ever get better at it? Will I find that special someone?*

I felt like two different people. My outward presentation of confidence and strength was no match for my inner battle.

I still wonder, as an older version of myself, if my college crush was the one who got away.

72 // NO MERCY

The miles felt like a slow crawl as I headed north to Phoenix after finishing play on Sunday at the Welch's-Circle K Championship in Tucson. Exhaustion settled over me as the high from my tie for sixth place dissipated. Thankfully, driving into Scottsdale felt familiar since I had lived there for six months with my sister and Loopy during the fall of 1994 and winter of 1995. Now in 1997, my sister still lived there six months out of the year when she wasn't in Vermont, and she was going to be my "housing" for the week.

My four sub-par rounds in Tucson added up to nine under par and a decent paycheck. I hit the ball well, but silly mental errors struck again. The difference throughout the tournament at Randolph Park Golf Course, however, was that I scrambled well and saved par when I needed to. I maintained my composure and played hard to the seventy-second hole. This had not always been my experience. One of my consistent struggles was not giving up after a few bad holes.

Professional golf shows no mercy. Every day I was reminded, *I am only as good as my last round*. I remember a particular round at Twelve Bridges Golf Course in Rockville, California, being my worst showing during my first three years on tour. When I saw my name only a few spots up from the bottom of the leaderboard, a wave of humiliation smacked me in the face.

The round was a comedy show. In total, I struck forty putts. Ridiculously fast greens bamboozled me to two four-putts and a couple three-putts. The absurdity partially cooled my anger. The best choice I had was to be objective, accept the circumstance, and continue on. One round didn't define who I was or what I could accomplish the next day. The ink on my journal page accepted it—*but did I really believe it?*

Truth be told, feeling like a failure smoldered like flames resting under warm coals.

My nerves were shot. My life revolved around my ability to play golf. I was barely hanging on to the pedestal that I perceived I was thrust upon by my family, my caddies, my friends. I had little proof to believe differently.

Fear of failing and fear of winning conjoined. *Why can't I be focused and aggressive?* Playing golf defensively only created more frustration.

Most weeks I suppressed my fears and pressed on. The 1997 U.S. Women's Open at Pumpkin Ridge Golf Club in Beaverton, Oregon, snatched my attention for a couple reasons. My mom would be with me for the week and I loved any chance I had to return and play back in the Pacific Northwest where I played all of my junior golf.

Mom enjoyed ironing my golf clothes and I loved having her pigeon-toed waddle and cheers in the gallery. As each day of the week progressed, I noticed she complained about having a headache every day. And something was different about her face, but I didn't quite know what.

The U.S. Women's Open always demanded accuracy off the tee box. The thick rough on both sides of the fairways at Pumpkin Ridge was no joke. Over the course of the first two rounds, I missed more fairways than I hit and found myself scrambling for pars. I also had very few birdie opportunities. This combination made for a long, exhausting first two rounds.

I managed to make the two-day cut, but my frustration with my driver had boiled over and I had to do something about it. I needed to take that driver out of my bag so I would not be tempted to use it during the weekend rounds. I did take it out and even went one step further: I had my caddy physically break the shaft in half. I relegated myself to using my three-wood off the tee on Saturday and Sunday. It was not ideal at all, but I found some momentum in my swing, and after hitting more fairways on Sunday, I finished with a seventy-two.

I carried two Scripture passages in my yardage book, a pocket-size map of each hole on the course with yardages from different points of reference, hazards, and pictures of the greens where we (player and caddy) added notes about the course.

The first verse was 2 Timothy 1:7.

"For God gave us a spirit not of fear but of power and love and self-control."

The second one was Hebrews 10:35-36.

"Therefore, do not throw away your confidence, which has a great reward. For you have need of endurance, so that when you have done the will of God you may receive what is promised."

Meditating on God's Word between shots seemed to help me stay present and to let go of the outcome. But, the practice did feel a little like a Band-Aid. My fear and anxiety were not helping me, but I didn't know how to shake them off.

It was important to me to play well in front of my Pacific Northwest crowd. I believed God had given me the talent to play professional golf; I wanted His glory to shine through me. My goal for the week was to keep my attention centered in the present—to stay within myself and be a good witness. There were good moments of doing so, and I still had a lot of emotional and mental growth to do.

Despite my persistent fear and anxiety on the course, in my first three years on Tour, I made my first hole-in-one, shot a career-low sixty-three, made over $100,000 each year, and easily retained my tour exemption. And, I journeyed through a cross-country move, a broken engagement, a re-injured back, and the hardest days of my life.

73 // A ROUND WITH NANCY LOPEZ

I gulped when I saw my pairing for the fourth and final round of the Rochester International: Nancy Lopez. *The* Nancy Lopez. The Hall of Fame legend and three-time winner at this very tournament in Rochester, New York. Nancy was the queen of this course and community, and I was paired with her.

Torrential rain had already washed out an entire day of play at the tournament. Rounds one and two were pushed into Saturday, and I sloshed my way through the final twelve holes of round three on Sunday morning. I completely lost track of the number of stoppages. I barely had time to eat and warm-up again before the start of round four.

Thankfully, the sun finally emerged, and the temperature settled into the mid-seventies. A welcome reprieve from the previous days' weather. At least I had that going for me.

I walked nervously to the first tee Sunday afternoon for round four, muttering to my caddy, "I'm pretty sure all these people aren't here to watch me play today." To which my caddy responded, *Duh!* (Not out loud), but I could tell that's what he was thinking. I was so nervous.

Nancy greeted me on the first tee. It wasn't the first time we had met, but I felt small in her presence. Her smile brought a small amount of ease to my nerves, but playing with her was not going to be easy.

The crowd had gathered two and three people deep behind the fairway ropes all the way down the first hole. I should have realized what might be ahead. I was but a shadow against their adopted hometown golf hero.

Every time Nancy took a shot, the fans stood still as statues. And the second her ball lifted into the air, those same fans were on the move, making sure they didn't miss a moment of play. Each hole felt like a fight. My imagination wrote a tagline that it didn't matter that I was in this group.

I sat down exhausted to check over our scorecards. The weight of disappointment with my performance began to ooze through me at my final score of seventy-six. I watched my name fall down the leaderboard.

Nancy played round four with grace, and it appeared that the large crowds only intensified her focus. Whereas I was distracted from the get-go. I played fearfully and anxiously, letting Nancy's celebrity status and her crowd of followers distract me from my game.

Another life lesson learned on the tour. It didn't matter who I was paired with or who was watching. The president of the United States could be standing in the gallery and my job remained the same: stay focused and play fiercely.

74 // THE JUNIOR CLINIC

The turnout was small, as I expected. Junior golf at TLV was not high on the list of sport activities. Regardless, I agreed to host a clinic. My community had supported me in my journey to the LPGA, despite a few doubters, and it was important to me to give back.

As the parents and kids started to gather, I didn't notice them right away. When I did, I went mute. "Uh, uh, hey… oh… hi," I muttered, cringing and forcing a smile. Coach and his wife smiled back and introduced their son and daughter who scurried off to find a lump of golf balls to hit.

We kicked off the clinic with me hitting balls for the kids as the head golf professional from TLV narrated my movements. I hit low and high shots. I made the ball curve left to right and then right to left. The ball exploded off my driver and the kids cheered enthusiastically. Inside, I was walking an emotional tightrope.

After a short break, the kids spread out to hit balls themselves. The head pro and I started at opposite ends to work our way from one junior golfer to the next. Some needed to be shown how to hold the club while others showed off their fundamental skills.

There was no choice—I *had* to help every young person who was at the clinic. It made sense to the community that Coach would bring his kids. His son and daughter were being kids, wanting to hit golf balls and meet Miss Tracy.

My vision blurred, blurring the lingering parents into the background. *Focus on the kids,* I repeated. *Focus on the kids.* In my peripheral vision, I noticed the Coeur d'Alene Press sports reporter snapping photographs, but I thought nothing of it.

The following day, still recovering from the previous twenty-four hours, I needed to put the events of the clinic behind me. But when I walked into the kitchen with the morning paper laid out on the table, the sports page hit me like a sledgehammer. In disbelief, I stared at the featured picture: me helping Coach's daughter.

I thought I was okay. Yet, here I was—shaking and swallowing the secret again.

75 // THE WORLD IS SPINNING

Anger, frustration, disappointment. *Embarrassment.*

I played my way right out of the cut at the 1997 Safeway LPGA Golf Championship in Portland, Oregon; there was no Sunday round. Dad, my friend and the Softspikes tour rep Jeff, and the Thuns, who have become one of my favorite host families and family friends on tour, knew to stay out of my way when I exited the scoring tent. I gave obligatory hugs and made a beeline for the locker room. I needed space to calm down.

I grabbed all my junk from the locker and headed for the parking lot. Kenny, my caddy, was waiting for me with my bag by the car. His frustration was palpable too. It was early September already and the season was almost over. Instead of climbing up the money list, I was starting to drop in ranking.

I told Kenny I would touch base with him later. I found my dad and told him I was going to hang out with Jeff for the afternoon and I would see him for dinner.

I made myself call home. "Hi Mom. I missed the cut today," I said. Mom was home by herself. She was planning to join me the following week for my next tournament in Seattle.

"Okay, honey," she responded simply. "I'll talk to you later." Then she hung up.

Staring at the phone, my heart started to pound. *Something is not right.*

I dialed Mom back, but she didn't answer. The minutes ticked by slowly. "Think, Tracy," I whispered to myself. "Call Mary next door and ask her to go over and check things out."

Jeff and I decided to head to the movie theater, a great escape for my mixed-up emotions, and find a payphone there to call Mary back. The early September sun was still hot as I picked up the handle of the payphone. Mary answered. She spoke words I never thought I would hear: "I think Marcella had a stroke. I'm calling an ambulance."

I panicked. *What should I do?* Call Dad, then Debbie. *Find a flight. Get home.*

Jamie, my sweet friend who had taken me to my first junior golf tournament, picked me up from the airport and drove me to the Coeur d'Alene Hospital. I was surprised and grateful to see Bruce English standing outside of Mom's room when I arrived. As a local funeral director, Bruce happened to be in the hospital at the time the ambulance arrived. The Englishes and my family had sporadic contact over the twenty years since we had moved to TLV from Post Falls. Shaking, I instinctively buried my face into his chest and started sobbing. Dad was still a few hours away, driving from Portland.

"Are you ready?" Bruce asked. "I'll stay right here."

Jamie stayed, too.

My knees went weak. I held my breath as I crossed the threshold into the hospital room. The woman lying there couldn't be my *mom*. She looked like my grandmother—frail, sunken, small. Her right eye turned to me, but the left side of her face drooped, frozen.

I'm not ready to lose my mom, I thought weakly. *She's got so much more to live for*. Shock stifled my tears. *I'm scared. Be strong, no matter the cost.*

I grabbed her right hand. "I'm here, Mom."

The diagnosis was bad. Two brain tumors. One emergency surgery was needed now, and another was down the road, the doctors told us.

The next two days were a blur. Debbie arrived and Mom went into surgery. As Debbie and I sat with her, Mom groggily recounted that she saw four spirits during her surgery. She thought she had died. "I think God gave you four angels last night, Mom," I said as I held her hand. I was tired, as was my sister. My tears welled but never crested.

I could hardly bear to look at Mom without my heart exploding. Brain surgery and the cancer had done permanent damage. She would never again be the same person I'd always known. Her prognosis was not good. It was terminal.

The decision to stay home one more week came at a cost. I withdrew from a second tournament—one I had been looking forward to playing. I knew I was doing the right thing, though. I wanted to be with Mom, to help her get settled back at home and focus on healing. Mom needed me. Debbie needed me.

Dad? It was hard to tell. He seemed absent and hadn't been much help.

One evening, I cornered him behind his desk (his home office was set up in the living room) and begged him to spend more time with Mom. He turned defensive and stood up to leave, but I grabbed his keys before he could. I was so angry. He had already been drinking his nightly Bud Light and I wasn't going to let him go anywhere. We stood at a stalemate, face to face. As I saw his hands raise, I thought he was going to push me, but he just sat back down.

Dad always thought we had a good relationship solely because we are father and daughter. He was clueless. *Blood alone doesn't make a relationship.* My heart slowed. Taking a breath, I mustered, "Mom needs you. We need you."

He stared back at me in silence. I turned around and went to the other side of the house to cool off.

I hated that I saw a lot of myself in my dad—closed-off, defensive, speechless. But, that night, I was proud of myself for standing up to him and telling Dad what I thought about his behavior.

76 // A SPECIAL VISITOR

Mom's second surgery in early November was mostly successful. They extracted the majority of the second tumor, but were unable to get clear margins. More spots showed up on other areas of the brain. As her headaches continued to increase, Mom had good days and bad days. I traveled back and forth from Florida to Idaho as much as I could throughout my off season, but I also needed to focus on practicing come January for the start of the 1998 Tour season, which included a return to play the Hawaiian Open near Honolulu, Hawaii.

February is prime whale-watching in the South Pacific, and it just so happens to coincide with our LPGA event in Oahu. With the reality setting in that time was not on our side, my sister and I started asking Mom what she would like to see and do. One of her wishes was to see the whales in Hawaii. Mom needed to get out of North Idaho, so the trip would be a win-win scenario, in my book. The timing worked perfectly: Mom was going to join me in Hawaii on the last day of my event and then we would venture over to explore Maui for a few days together.

I played well the first two days of the tournament and was anxious as I awaited Mom's arrival to Hawaii. The knot in my gut grew tighter with each glance down at my watch. *Where was she? Did she make it through her layover in San Francisco?*

I managed my way through the first nine holes of my third round, but concern for my mom's safe arrival proved stronger than my golf focus. I tried to hide it, but I sensed my caddy's agitation. If all went right, the tournament transportation was going to pick Mom up after she landed and bring her over to the course. *She might even get to watch me play the last few holes*, I hoped. Scanning the horizon, I swallowed my rising heartbeat. *She's going to be fine.*

When I finally saw her, a wave of relief flooded my body. Shoving my tears back into the safety of my chest, I skirted out of my way to give her a hug, her face even more rounded from the meds than the last time I saw her. Disappointment in my final round of seventy-five was eclipsed by the fact that Mom *made it*.

The flight over to Maui went up and down before we could blink. "This is beautiful," I said quietly. Mom nodded; she looked tired. I proposed that she rest for a bit while I get the lay of the land.

The timeshare resort where we would stay was nestled in a quiet cove north of Lahaina. After booking two different whale-watching trips (one on a sailboat and one on a bigger boat), I wandered the property until I found the beach. My heart joined the rhythm of the lapping waves as my toes squished the heavy sand with each step.

Mom planned our four days on the island around food. As an enthusiastic coffee lover, she enjoyed the Hawaiian-brewed taste of Maui and Kona beans. Our taste buds danced their way through pastries, fruits of the tropics, and South Pacific fare. I wanted to be fully present, but I felt stuck between enjoying each moment with her and watching cautiously to make sure she was okay.

The heat and activity zapped Mom of her energy. While she napped in the afternoons, I meandered back to the quiet beach. On my third visit, I meandered along the curve where the water met the sand; small rocks rolling in and out with the waves caught my attention. I reached down for one and noticed it was much different from the typical jagged volcanic rocks that dotted the beach. This rock, and hundreds of others like it, was smooth and rounded. The perpetual circling of saltwater moving in and out of that little cove must have tamed its rough edges. I turned the stone over and over in my hand. The small, consistent waves had taken something sharp and made it soft and beautiful.

I felt the Holy Spirit's nudge of love toward me. *Like these stones, God works in our lives in a similar way. Little by little, as we open more of ourselves up to Him, He softens our rough edges—allowing us to grow into the beautiful vessels He created us to be.* My rough edges were still plenty sharp and needed some smoothing.

My heart skipped. I scavenged to find anything similar written in the Scriptures. I started in the concordance with a search for the word "smooth." My fingers moved quickly over chunks of pages until I found Isaiah 42:16.

"And I will lead the blind in a way that they do not know, in paths that they have not known I will guide them. I will turn the darkness before them into light, the rough places into level ground. These are the things I do, and I do not forsake them."

I sat in awe.
"I need this to be true, God," I whispered.

77 // THE LAST TIME

It was Friday, March 20, 1998, a bright, sunny day in Phoenix, Arizona. It had been nearly six months since my mom's diagnosis, and I was warming up for my afternoon tee-time at the Standard Register Ping LPGA Championship. My parents and I were staying with Debbie and her boyfriend, Rich. It was not often that both my sister and I were in the same location these days, let alone the whole family. Everyone was going to walk along the ropes. Well, except Mom, who would be in a disability scooter to navigate the golf course.

Instead of her bright smile and enthusiasm, I saw a weary, defeated, blank face.

After a nominal first-day score, I found my attention focused throughout the second round not only on my golf, but on my mom. My heart ached with overwhelming emotions: joy, sadness, gratitude. In an odd way, the distractions helped me play more freely and I shot a sixty-five: my best round of the season. Although I knew she didn't experience it fully with me, it was a gift for me that Mom could be there.

Mom was my biggest cheerleader and had always loved traveling to tournaments with me. Back in the day, she saw everything from the first tee shot to the last putt. Her high-pitched screams accompanied every birdie I made. The same scream I remember hearing from the bleachers during basketball games. Outwardly embarrassed, but inwardly proud, I always enjoyed looking into the crowd and finding her smile beaming back at me.

The stark contrast between the excitement of trying to win the golf tournament and the pain of watching my mom suffer was almost too much to bear. I didn't know for sure, but I felt this would probably be the last tournament she would ever watch me play.

Having Mom in the gallery and shooting a sixty-five is a treasure I still hold today. I wish I could say it was a gentle reminder that there was more to life than golf. But my golf performance continued to be the barometer for how and what I believed about myself.

78 // MOM'S LAST WORDS

"I'm going to get off the phone now," my mom said to me.

"Mom, tell me you love me," I asked.

"I love you, honey."

"Okay, Mom, I'll talk to you tomorrow."

"Okay, goodbye."

I sat back on the couch and spun our conversation over and over in my head. It was May, two months after the Phoenix tournament, and Mom didn't feel like talking for long. That was the new norm. It also struck me that I had never had to ask her to tell me she loved me before. With all our family's emotional dysfunction, we had still ended every phone call with an "I love you." Yet, for some reason this time, something in my spirit felt like she wasn't going to say it. Something in me just knew that I needed to hear her words.

The next day I understood why.

Six days prior, I had been wheeling Mom around Victoria Island in British Columbia, Canada, because she wanted to attend high tea at the Empress Hotel. As we (my mom, sister, and aunt) drank tea and ate sandwich wedges, Mom's vacant eyes, bloated face, and labored breathing were in stark contrast to the beautiful surroundings.

Mom was in her ninth month of fighting melanoma cancer and her body was deteriorating. Denial that the end was near wrestled my anxiety. After our weekend on the island, I asked my parents and sister if they wanted me to stay home instead of rejoining the LPGA Tour in Rochester, New York. They insisted I go, so I did.

Tour life often means thousands of miles of separation from my loved ones. In golf speak, it is par for the course. But this time leaving was excruciating.

I made it a point to call her every day, but it didn't assuage my growing anxiety. My first round in Rochester was a trainwreck and my old back injury flared with a vengeance. So much so that I withdrew from the tournament before the start of the second round—a first in my professional career. My body was coming to grips with what my mind could not. Things were not okay.

My conversations with Mom became shorter and shorter as each day of the week passed. After hanging up the phone on this night I didn't sense danger, but something still prompted me to make the request:

"Mom, tell me you love me."

Why would I spontaneously ask her that?

A day passed and my phone rang. My sister's voice cracked and mumbled through her tears, "She's gone."

"What?" I managed to whisper. I swallowed my breath speechless and paralyzed. My sister described the horrors of Mom's final hours: 911, paramedics, and violent attempts at resuscitation. I was drowning in regret. I should have been there. I should never have left. I should have . . .

The next few hours whirled by with tears and phone calls. Mom was gone. May 31, 1998.

Our last conversation the night before compressed my thoughts.

"Mom, tell me you love me."

"I love you, honey."

These were the last words I heard my mom say. The hurt and pain from Mom's death has and continues to heal over time. Even so, the month of May can still feel hard. Sadly, my mom's voice has faded in my memory, and I struggle to hear its pitch and tone.

However, I hold this gift God gave me.

"I love you, honey."

79 // BOUND TO THE LIE

My poem lacked professional creativity, but it accurately reflected the ambivalence choking my heart. *Will I be able to read it out loud?* I dug deep for the courage to face the day. May 31, 1998, Mom's funeral.

Hiding behind the wall separator, my family and I waited for the ceremony to begin. A roller coaster of chills moved up and down my body. We all fidgeted. *What was taking so long?* Peeking around the corner, I scanned the room, which overflowed with people. A face caught my eye, and I did a double take.

He was here, on the back wall, with his wife. He looked at me and nodded.

I quickly ducked back behind the separator, my heart in my stomach. I couldn't *believe* that Coach had come. It took everything in me to keep my composure. Only my sister Sheli and a couple friends knew about the "relationship" with him; everyone else—including my family—would expect him to show up to support me.

Sitting in the front row, I pressed my tears away and shivered. Was this what an out-of-body experience feels like? *I am here but I'm not here.* The pastor leading the service didn't really know my mom and his words felt empty. He gave me the nod and I swallowed my tears as I walked up to the platform. I robotically read my poem. (I've included it in the back of the book.) And then it was over.

Our family was led to the next room over for the dreaded receiving line and reception. *I don't want to greet Coach. I just want him to leave me alone.* Once again I had no choice. I don't remember what he said or if I replied. I'm sure I stood rigid, wearing a fake smile. The nausea mixed with the misery I already was feeling because of Mom. And now, keeping watch over *the secret* took precedent even at my mom's funeral.

80 // ASK AND YOU WILL RECEIVE

"Would you like to pray for the group before the evening session begins?" the camp director, Rock, asked me.

Was this a joke? Yes, I had asked God several months ago to help me become a better pray-er. But not right now, at this moment, standing in front of several hundred middle school and high school students at the all-sports Fellowship of Christian Athletes summer camp. Rock didn't know me, he just knew I was a professional athlete in attendance, and how cool it would be to have her—me—pray for everyone. Terrified, I froze and declined the invitation.

"You said 'no'?" my friend asked, with a hint of disappointment and surprise.

Shame was mounting.

"Well, Rock's request took me by surprise, and I blurted out 'no,'" I responded defensively.

Since Mom's death a few months earlier, I had little desire to read my Bible or talk to God about anything. I wasn't mad at Him per se, I just was numb to everything. That, coupled with how much I disliked talking in front of people and the fact that praying has never been a gift of mine—I perceive I never have the right words—made me a terrible candidate to lead the group with prayer.

But as soon as the words came out of my mouth, a familiar pit in my stomach grew. I felt defensive because the Holy Spirit was nudging me to do it, "You asked to learn how to pray better. Now's the time!"

Rock's invitation was significant. It's one of those "I know I should but I really don't want to" situations. I navigated my way back to Rock and told him that I had changed my mind, and I would open up the session with prayer.

I firmly gripped the podium, took a big breath, and looked out into the crowd of teenagers and adults. I prayed for the campers, the staff, and the speaker … at least I'm pretty sure I did. Between my nerves and the sweat dripping down my back, I did it. I exhaled and gave myself an imaginary victory fist bump as I walked back to my seat.

In the years hence, I have still wrestled with praying. I'm not one to sit for long periods of time working through a list. I liken my prayer life to an all-day walk with the Lord. I admit, I often miss the Spirit's cues and attempt to figure things out on my own. But my spirit continues to grow more attuned to God's voice every day and while I may not be the first to offer to pray in a group, saying "yes" when asked was getting easier.

81 // NEW LIFE

As she snuggled into me, I snuggled deeper into the couch. The weight of her little body warmed my chest. Exhaustion overtook me and I melted away into dreamland.

My body's twitch startled me awake. A split second passed, and I relaxed gazing at my first-born niece Haley. She was beautiful and an indescribable love captured me.

I hadn't made it to Vermont for Haley's birth due to the LPGA Tour schedule, but I arrived as quickly as possible. She was only two weeks old and so fragile. I was scared to change her diaper for fear I might hurt her.

Debbie and Rich married in October of 1999, a year after we lost Mom. About nine months later they named their firstborn after her: Haley Marcella. They settled in southern Vermont full time. No more back and forth to Phoenix for the winter months.

I had no anticipation for how much Debbie's child would rock my world. I only had one week to hold Haley as much as possible. My sister had natural mothering instincts. I needed to watch and learn how to swaddle, coo, and cradle Haley. I was smitten.

I didn't want to leave this precious, little girl who had brought life back into my grieving heart.

82 // NATIONAL TRAGEDY

More than a year had passed. The 2001 Tour season was only weeks away from concluding, which was hard for me to believe. I shifted into park and the car rocked a little before completely stopping. My mood for the day agreed with the sky—a deep, gloomy Oregon gray. Another Tuesday practice round loomed. With a long exhale, I jumped out of the car. The locker room was unusually quiet. I scooped myself a bowl of hot oatmeal as a quick breakfast before my caddy started looking for me.

I turned the corner to find a seat and saw others' eyes locked on the television screen, mouths agape in horror. *What's happening? Is this a movie?* Two tall buildings bellowed with smoke. Headlines flashed: *New York. Planes. Towers. People jumping.* An eerie silence filled the space as we attempted to digest what we were watching. Then, the unthinkable happened. One building collapsed. Then, the second. Silence.

Waking up three hours behind New York in the Pacific time zone, we joined the rest of the United States in shock at the devastation of the 9/11 terrorist attacks. Those of us at the golf course paced the locker room. *What do we do now?* Playing golf felt petty, but, on the other hand, it was what we knew. We all felt uncertain, horror-struck, nauseous.

As I walked around in aimless circles outside, the sky was silent. This might've been the eeriest thing.

Columbia Edgewater Country Club was only a few miles from Portland International Airport. Normally, all day, every day, planes ascended and descended directly over the course as we walked the fairways. I got used to the noise after the first couple days, especially as fighter jets rumbled through the afternoon skies. But, that morning on September 11, 2001, *nothingness.* All planes in North America, we learned, were grounded until further notice.

I didn't play golf that day or the rest of the week. Like most other professional sports leagues, our tournament sponsors canceled the event by Wednesday, which was the right thing to do. One hundred and forty-four LPGA golfers and their tour caddies—me included—were stuck in Portland, Oregon, with no idea how we will travel 2,700 miles across the country to make our next event in North Augusta, South Carolina.

Some grabbed the few remaining rental cars and started the long drive east. The rest of us sat and waited. Our Christian Fellowship group put together a prayer service for a time to be together amid the tragedy. Collectively sharing our sadness and sorrow brought a short reprieve to what felt like an escalating unknown. Stories of personal connections to the tragedy were shared. We prayed and wept. I'm grateful for how our international LPGA golf community came together when hard things happened.

As the week passed very slowly, planes were still grounded, and our anxiety increased. *When will we be able to travel again? Will it be safe? Are we going to play next week?*

The tournament organizers went above and beyond to help us. Once the prohibition to fly was lifted, they agreed to divert half of the tournament purse money toward a chartered flight for players, family, and caddies. Those choosing to fly on the plane will pay the other half of the cost. It was a good plan—even if it was the only available plan at this point.

I was very grateful for Dave and Mary Lou Thun. They had become like family and their peaceful home was a respite amidst the tension of the week.

The Thuns dropped another player staying with them, Lori, and me off at the private airport terminal. LPGA staff, players, and caddies gathered; conversations remained quiet throughout the security process. The sun warmed the cool September air as it bounced off the concrete tarmac. We shuffled towards the stairway leading up to the 737 spanning before us. One by one, we boarded. Everything was going according to plan: we were getting out of Portland.

Tensions were still high, especially getting on a plane again. There were still many unknowns regarding the 9/11 terrorist attacks. "Breathe. We're going to be okay," I whispered to my seatmates.

By the time we reached Augusta, Georgia, it was late, but we didn't care. Solid ground beneath our feet felt wonderful. Exhausted, we fell into tournament transportation vehicles for the twenty-minute drive to hotels and housing across the border in North Augusta.

Our nation was still reeling a week after the 9/11 attacks, and recovery efforts were still in full force. The tournament served as a much-needed distraction from reality, and I found solace walking the fairways with my caddy and fellow LPGA peers. I also played my best golf of the season. On Sunday, I had a chance to win but an untimely bogey on the second to last hole resulted in a second-place finish.

My best payday of my career offered a reprieve amid our national tragedy.

83 // NOW THERE ARE TWO

The weeks after the 9/11 attacks were a blur. The golf season finished, and I was back in Vermont to babysit Haley while we waited for her sister to join the world. Debbie was put on light bed rest during the last month, and she had been going stir crazy. But most likely Courtney Ann would arrive before her projected due date.

I told Debbie that whatever it takes, she had better not give birth on Halloween. She dutifully obliged and Courtney arrived on November 1. Whereas Haley took after Debbie and my mom's side of the family, Courtney had the Hanson genes. Blonde and blue-eyed, she could have been as much my daughter as my sister's.

To be honest, I considered the girls like my own, and still do. The best part was I got to play, spoil, and then give them back to their parents. The best of both worlds. I didn't think I could love another child as much as I loved Haley, but it turned out I was wrong. Now I had two little girls to love. I almost couldn't contain it.

I was going to be the best aunt ever!

84 // THREE?

"I'm pregnant again." Debbie's stuttered words exposed her fears.

I paused and spoke carefully. I wanted to say *Congratulations! I can't wait to be an aunt again!* But I knew. I knew she was exhausted with having two babies in less than two years, along with a job and a new house project. I exhaled.

"I know this feels like a lot. And you're going to be okay. How's Rich feeling about it?"

Rich had been wanting to try for a third child because he wanted a boy. I too would love to have a nephew. Then good news came. André was on his way. The best of both worlds—two girls and a boy.

Months passed and time was drawing near for André's due date. Once again Debbie was sequestered to bed rest. The doctors predicted another early birth. I took the State Farm Classic off since the Illinois tourney would have tied me up when I wanted to be able to take care of the girls while Debbie and Rich were at the hospital.

The stars aligned. On the first of September, two days before I needed to leave for the next LPGA event in Oklahoma I got the call from Rich that André Thomas arrived to complete our family. The girls jumped up and down. Haley's two-year-old self understood another baby was coming home. Courtney, who was one month shy of a year, was in for an awakening. She would no longer be the baby of the family.

The girls and André were reminders that we could love again even after all our recent losses. But of course, more grief would come again.

85 // LOSING SHELI

"Sheli, I love you."

I whispered my final words to my sister as her mom, Cheryl, held the other end of the phone to Sheli's ear. I don't know if she heard me or not, but I hoped she did.

Sinking into my couch, I sobbed. Death was once again on our doorstep. Numbness enveloped me as I waited.

Unsure of how much time had passed, my phone rang and startled me out of my trance. "Sheli's gone," whispered Cheryl. Twenty-eight hundred miles away, my sister had drawn her last breath.

Three women in my family over five years have been taken by cancer. *Mom. Elaine. Sheli.*

Our wild, red-headed, extroverted Aunt Elaine, who married my mom's brother Eddie, lost her battle with breast cancer two and a half years after Mom passed. Elaine was an instigator. For example, I picked up the Ping Pong paddle and accepted her challenge to play. Little did I know that she had game, and my ego proved no match for her competitive spirit. She pushed my buttons like no other human being alive, and she also loved me deeply. She was a ray of light to our family.

Now it was Sheli, my half-sister, five years my senior. I looked at the calendar, Monday, March 3, 2003. I was supposed to fly to Tucson, Arizona, the following week for the first week of a four-week swing on the LPGA Tour. Sheli's memorial service was to be held in five days, on Saturday, in Rocklin, California. I needed to practice; I needed to pack; *I needed to get to California.*

As a corporate travel agent and my travel coordinator, Sheli taught me savvy travel skills. I quickly went to work, changing my plans. I couldn't believe she was gone.

Debbie will meet me in Rocklin, and, together, we'll help Cheryl with the memorial service, I formulated. Immediately after, I would fly to Tucson for the tournament.

Sheli came into this world during Dad's first marriage. Sheli loved life despite living in the crosshairs of divorced parents and a blended family. Her gregarious personality changed any frown into a smile, and she consistently pushed aside her emotional trauma. I have sporadic memories with Sheli as kids. She spent some holidays with us, but she never accepted my invitation to watch me play basketball. I didn't understand her heartache, nor she mine, until we forged our own relationship outside of our parents as adults.

Sheli jumped fashion styles like a thief in the night. One year, it was a sports car and R&B. Six months later, her blonde hair and blue eyes preferred Wranglers, cowboy boots, and a hat. The sports car became a Ford. Her hairstyles followed suit, from short and lopsided to long and curly. During chemo, she sported a beautiful buzz cut and wigs.

Sheli was one person who pulled me out of my shell on many occasions—nights out dancing and national rodeos, included. Her infectious zest for life turned her pain into an upbeat, positive attitude. She worked hard and played hard. She is forever my sister.

On the day Sheli got married, I should've been more excited for her. Instead, dread nestled close by because she had asked Debbie to sing and me to accompany on guitar. It was a ludicrous request, really—I wasn't a guitarist by any stretch of the imagination. I only dabbled. To Sheli, that was just a minor detail. On top of my wavering talent, Debbie had never sung with a guitar accompaniment before, and we had to do the gig outdoors. Wearing a western skirt and cowboy boots as a bridesmaid also stretched my fashion world.

With every ounce of my internal focus and willpower, I finger-picked my way along while Debbie sang like an angel. Sheli's wide, bright smile and tears thanked us.

Only for my sister—my one and only guitar performance.

My plans came together for the funeral. We made it through, but another piece of my heart shattered.

86 // ON-COURSE ANTICS

I cruised around the course in a mediocre trance, another round in another city. I wasn't playing poorly, per se, but nothing spectacular flowed through me, either. It was a ho-hum golf day. I zeroed in on my yardage; a simple seven iron to the middle of the green. The small gallery sprinkled around the course watched expectantly. Before my arms reached the end of my swing, I *knew*. The ball launched immediately left into the air, soaring over the far greenside bunker.

"Fore!" we yelled in unison. But it was fruitless so far away—the ball made contact in the audience. I cringed and my heart dropped into my stomach. My caddy shrugged and started down the fairway. *Ugh, I hope that person is okay*, I thought.

I found my ball left of the green in the light rough. Not a bad lie at all. I also found the woman who took the hit.

"I'm so sorry about hitting you," I apologized profusely. Luckily, the ball had bounced once before it ricocheted off her leg. She smiled and waved off my concern. "I'm fine, really," she said kindly.

I took a deep breath and apologized again, joking about how she helped keep me in play. We laughed together and I turned toward the green to analyze my next shot.

After finishing the hole, I walked back over to the woman and tossed her my ball.

A small memento and gesture to help me continue my round.

Another moment etched in my memory happened at the Sybase Big Apple Classic at Wykagyl Country Club in New York. My approach shot into the green had missed and nestled in the heavy rough on the right. A downhill, fast-sloping green stared back at me. My only chance to keep my ball on the green was to hit a flop shot. The margin for error was *zero*.

I posed in my half follow-through but saw no ball in the air. I knew I'd hit the grass. My head darted to the ground and then up to my caddy. What the heck just happened? Bending over for a closer look, I found my ball in the same place it had been before—just a little deeper.

Did I just whiff? Several seconds passed before my senses came back online. My club went clean under the ball. The heat of embarrassment rushed down my spine. I had to add a stroke for the whiff and had to hit the same frightening shot again. My second attempt popped out of the rough and landed on the green. At least I had a putt for bogey.

After playing tournament golf for over four decades, I'm still learning that the game is not about pursuing perfection, something I have struggled with in many areas of my life. Trying to be perfect was a way to quiet my shame that I wasn't enough, that I wasn't damaged and broken.

And that drive to perform was always being upended by highs and lows on the tour—some funny, some beyond difficult.

The sweltering St. Louis heat was no joke as we plotted our way around the course on the final round of the Michelob Light Classic. The two-story, air-conditioned sponsor tents around number eighteen were some of the largest I had seen.

Playing well and near the lead, my heart rate quickened as I walked up to the eighteenth tee box. One more birdie would cap off a solid round. *Get your drive in the fairway, Tracy.* The crack of the ball against my driver felt toward the toe. *Oh no … not left!*

Everything in me wanted to slam my driver hard to the ground. I made the motion but stopped before impact. I speed-walked myself off the tee box and toward my ill-placed fate in the trees to the left.

My caddy Kenny stood by the ball. Trees and the extravagant sponsor tents limited my sightline to the pin.

"Wait a second, Tracy," he gasped. "We can use the rules to our advantage here."

The rules of golf are complicated. Penalty areas: Add one stroke. Out of bounds: Add two strokes. Unplayable lie: One stroke. Temporary Immovable Obstructions: Line of sight, one-club length, and free drop. . .*Bingo*. That was one of those "right situations." My ticket out of tree jail.

I quickly called for a Rules Official and motioned my playing partners to carry on. Kenny and I started walking to the right until the sponsor tent was no longer in my line of sight. I was allowed one club length beyond that point to take my free drop no nearer to the hole.

From an impassable shot through the trees to an opening for a seven iron up to the green. Kenny and I were still laughing as we walked to the scorer's tent after my routine par.

87 // CHILLED TO THE BONE

Jeju Island—South Korea's southernmost island and a popular honeymoon destination—was one of my last events of the 2003 season. Fortunately for our wallets, the sponsors paid for business class airfare and hotel rooms. We couldn't bring our tour caddies, but the tournament provided local caddies, all of whom were females. I anticipated quiet walks around the course since none of them spoke English.

Like everyone else who traveled halfway around the world to play the event, I packed for mild fall weather, anticipating highs somewhere in the sixties.

Much to our dismay, Jeju Island was experiencing abnormally low temperatures. I panicked. I had forgotten my rain gear (a second layer of warmth even when there was no rain) and I had no hand warmers or winter cap. Word trickled around that the pro shop had beanie caps splashed with the New York Yankees logo. I beelined for the shop and barely grabbed one before they were snatched up by other shivering golfers. Thankfully, I nabbed a couple hand warmers, too.

After barely surviving days one and two, I caught wind that a friend had an extra pair of rain pants I could borrow. Praise God—the following day predicted even lower, bone-chilling temperatures with blowing wind.

I surveyed my wardrobe. My first layer will be thicker dress pants I wore to last night's sponsor dinner. Smiling, I noticed my pajama bottoms. *Why not?* I pulled the flannel pants on for layer number two. To complete my outfit, the oversized rain pants slid on easily. For my upper body, I triple-layered and added a jacket. My new Yankees beanie finished off the eclectic ensemble.

The eccentric layers helped but not enough. It wasn't just cold—it was bitter. Tears dripped from my eyes with every slap of the wind. Our golf balls oscillated on the greens. I couldn't feel my hands or toes. I desperately wanted to call it quits. *In fact, I am going to quit,* I thought, not even halfway through my round. *I can't take it anymore.* The bright sun deceived my senses and provided no relief.

It was, by far, the coldest round of golf I had ever played.

Hours passed before I thawed and felt the blood moving sluggishly through my body again. I had dug deep for every ounce of perseverance I could muster to finish the round.

I don't quit.

88 // ADVERSITY AND GRIT

"This is the biggest hotel room in England," I chirped. Dark wood wrapped around the room, minimizing the look of two double beds positioned across the left wall. The summer afternoon light peered through two large wood-framed windows off to the right. I always fretted about booking a hotel for the 2006 Women's British Open. This week, I was completely satisfied.

England's northwest coast held some familiarity; on it, I had played several courses. This week, the iconic Royal Lytham and St. Annes Golf Club was our muse. Known for its 167 bunkers, the links-style course required pinpoint accuracy with every stroke. The bunkers played no favorites. Miss your mark by a mere *yard* and one will swallow your ball. From tee to green, I was not safe until the ball clinked the bottom of the cup.

The weather was no joke, either. Unlike for the South Korea trip, I came prepared for everything and anything at any time—rain, wind, cold, sun, warmth. It wasn't even the first day of tournament play and we already had experienced the gamut of weather during our practice days.

Links-style golf is just plain *hard*, especially for those of us who grew up playing in North America. Rapidly changing elements, firm fairways, and large, slower-speed greens tests the patience of the best golfers in the world.

I did my prep and was as ready as I could be for the tournament rounds. The next item on my agenda was dinner and a 99 Flake ice cream cone before I called it a night. I had the afternoon/morning wave that week. (Every tournament, we played in the same groups of three for the first two rounds. If you played in the morning on Thursday, you would always play in the afternoon on Friday, and vice versa.) A good night's sleep and leisurely morning would put fuel in my tank for the quick turnaround.

A slight increase in the outside temperature mixed with moisture from the nearby sea made our room stuffy. The old windows in our room moved inversely; instead of pushing the bottom half of the window up to open it, the top half had to slide down the heavy frame. We needed some air, so my friend worked the left window into an open position before we wandered down for breakfast.

As I waited to head to the course for the first round of the 2006 Women's British Open, the open window caught my attention. *We should probably close that before we leave,* I thought. I had a whole conversation in my head as I waltzed over and climbed on an old chair for leverage to push the window up and lock it into place. I gave it a good heave with both hands. The latches were millimeters from clicking. Caught at an awkward angle, my left hand slipped *just enough*. I lost my hold and the window slammed down with a screeching crash.

"Help! HELP!" I screamed. Tears flooded my eyes. I couldn't move my left hand, crushed in the fallen frame. My friend came running out of the bathroom. "Push the window up! Push the window up! My finger!" I cried.

She jumped up on the same chair I was standing on and pushed with all her might. When my hand came free, I felt my knees go weak and my friend helped get both of us both safely to the floor. My left ring finger pulsated with pain and blood. Holding my wrist with my injury upright, my face went white with shock.

Several minutes passed before blood began to circulate in my brain again. The window survived while my hopes for the week slinked away. *Was it broken? How am I going to play golf in three hours?*

Ice is hard to come by in England, but, gratefully, the hotel found some. I needed to reach our athletic trainer immediately. I was desperate for a miracle. Maybe he could help me find one. First, we determined that it wasn't broken; good news. However, there was little give or bend happening under the swelling. Tucked in the recesses of his medical kit, we found several full-finger compression sleeves. I had no idea such a thing existed.

Slowly, gingerly, he rolled the sleeve down my finger. Every micro-movement sent chills down my spine. *Deep breath, Tracy. Deep breath. Deep breath.* After seconds that felt like minutes, the compression sleeve was on. I popped several ibuprofen to dull the pain, and we cut the matching finger off from my glove. I slid my injured hand tenderly through. *How on earth will I grip the club?*

I gently curled my four good fingers around the grip. My ring finger stuck straight out. "I think I have enough pressure to hold on to the club,"

I said. "I'll give it a go."

My afternoon was riddled with bogies and ibuprofen, but I completed all eighteen holes. There would be no practice afterward—only ice, pain medication, and sleep (if even possible).

Friday morning came quickly. The compression sleeve on my ring finger kept the swelling contained, but the throbbing pain was constant. I willed my way around the bunkers in round two, barely making the cut.

The swelling decreased with each passing day, but I still couldn't grip the club fully. I really can't tell you how I crept my way up the leaderboard over the last thirty-six holes. But somehow I left with a miraculous top-thirty finish.

Adversity and grit don't always have a happy ending. But my grit won at what ended up being my last Women's British Open.

89 // GOLF NIGHTMARES

I jumped out of the car and ran to the tee box. "Where's my golf bag?" I cried in a panic. No one seemed to care. My bare feet stared up at me. No clubs. No shoes. *Where is my caddy?*

The rules of golf declared that if I arrived within five minutes of my time, I could still tee off, join my playing partners down the first fairway, but I'd have to add a two-shot penalty. If I arrived after that five-minute post tee time window, then I would be disqualified from the event.

I had less than five minutes to find my shoes, caddy, and clubs. *Where are they?* I sprinted back to the clubhouse. Breathless gasps of air squeezed my heart and choked my lungs. *Why was no one answering me?*

I jerked upward in the dark room, startled. My entire body was tense and breathless. It had been a dream, but one that felt *so* real. My T-shirt clung to my damp skin as my head sunk back to my pillow.

I mulled around my room gathering my things for the first round of the LPGA Championship. It was still dark outside. I had plenty of time for my twenty-minute drive to the course. *Or, so I thought.* The phone rang. "Where are you?" said a frantic voice on the other end of the line. "Travis is freaking out."

"Oh, sh*t." My recurring golf nightmare had entered my reality.

I should have been at the course walking to the practice area at that very moment, not leaving my hotel room. My brain miscalculated. Grabbing everything in a heap, I ran to my car and proceeded to break every traffic law and speed limit. When I peeled into the golf course parking lot, Travis was waiting impatiently.

"I'm so sorry," I blurted out. "I'm so sorry. I messed up on the time." Shakily, I pulled on my golf shoes and jumped into the shuttle cart for the practice range. I had twenty minutes to warm up and get to the tee box. My whole body was shaking. My heart rate felt as though I was sprinting the last hundred meters of a race. *I need to breathe. Slow down, Tracy.*

Thankfully, I made it to the tee on time, but my mind was in an upheaval. Even though I am years removed from tournament golf —golf nightmares still populate my sleep state. When I played over twenty events each year, the fear of not calculating my pre-round timing with accurate precision haunted me. The nightmares come less often as I age, but they still play in the shadows of my mind when I least expect them.

90 // CADDIES

"I'll have a hot fudge sundae for my meal and a garden salad for dessert." Four faces stared blankly at Tat before I burst into laughter.

A server in America would shrug and move on. We weren't in America, however; we were in England. The server froze, not understanding if Tat was serious about her unconventional request.

"She's serious," I looked up with a smile.

It had been a long week at the Women's British Open and Tat, my caddy, had worked hard. In her opinion, life was too short: "Eat what you want and enjoy it!" Standing barely five-foot-four, Tat's confidence labored the bag around the course with grit and tenacity. She was a retired volleyball coach-turned-LPGA Tour caddy.

Tat was one of five different long-term caddies I had during my LPGA career. In addition to Tat there were Kenny, Big Nick, Lonnie, and Skyscraper (a.k.a.Jerry). I'm grateful for these professionals. Having a trusted caddy on the bag made tour life a little bit easier and a little less lonely.

On the LPGA Tour, there are tour caddies and local caddies. The tour caddies travel the full season; they either have a permanent "bag" (the same player they worked for each week) or they picked up one-week jobs. During my time on Tour, caddies had credentials and were vetted by players. Now they get background checks by the LPGA Tour. In many ways, tour caddies have a hierarchy just like the players do. As a caddy's player succeeds, so does the caddy's status.

Being a caddy was a long-suffering gig—it required showing up early and having patience to wait. A caddy must be ready when their player is ready. Good caddies know course strategy and learn how far their player hits each club down to the yard.

The job description included walking the course before I showed up onsite, being an encouragement, remaining calm under pressure, packing a nearly forty-pound tour bag, and getting wet in the rain in order to keep their player and clubs dry.

Some players solely wanted a bag carrier. My caddies, on the other hand, were my teammates. While any final decision rested on my shoulders, a good caddy made bad rounds better and provided guard rails when I played well.

I first met Kenny, a friend of a fellow alumni golfer from SJSU, when he approached me late on a Friday at my first Women's British Open in England. "Would I be interested in a tour caddy for the weekend?" he asked. Kenny's player had missed the cut, but I had made it to play on the weekend. Waves of tension rolled through me. If I said "yes," I would have to "fire" my local caddy when he hadn't done anything wrong. It would cost me more money, but what would I miss if I said "no?"

I knocked in my last putt on hole eighteen and shot an excited look over at Kenny. I just carded a third-round sixty-six. Kenny's experience calmed my nerves and helped lead me around Woburn Country Club with a better strategy than I had in my first two rounds. A day later, I walked away with a top-ten finish at the biggest event of my professional career to date. With Kenny's help, combined with the four tournaments I played earlier in the summer, my accumulative money list position on the 1994 European Ladies Tour earned me *Rookie of the Year*.

Ten months later, I hired Kenny as my first full-time tour caddy during my rookie year on the LPGA Tour. After working two and a half years together, frustration with one another led to Kenny making the decision to quit. This wasn't uncommon on tour—players fired caddies, and caddies fired players. Sometimes it's for good, but after a break, a player and caddy might reunite like Kenny and I did a couple seasons later.

My heart raced with anxiety as I sat down with Big Nick, a tall Hawaiian resident of Hungarian descent with a smile that drew you into a great big bear hug. Nick was special. When I had hired Kenny my first year on tour, Nick was the one I said "no" to. Most caddies would harbor resentment—not Nick. He was disappointed, but he wanted what was best for me. I never forgot his kindness, and he never treated me any differently.

For that reason, it was a no-brainer to call Nick at the beginning of my fourth year on tour and ask if he would caddy for me in Hawaii after Kenny and I went different ways. "If it goes well," I said, "it could be a permanent job." He said "yes" before I got all the words out. Nick was a caddy, big brother, and friend all wrapped up in one. He didn't take life too seriously and always told a great story. His servant heart cared for me during the season in which my mom battled her cancer, the hardest year of my life.

"Nick, how are you getting to Daytona?" He shrugged, not seeming too worried about it. "Would you want to drive with me through the night? It'll be a tough drive, but getting back to Ormond Beach"—where I now lived—"without wasting Monday would be great."

Ever-agreeable Nick cradled the steering wheel most of the eleven-hour drive from Nashville to Florida. I dozed on and off to his serenades of Frank Sinatra and the like. In the wee hours of the next morning, he was still telling stories as we pulled into Ormond Beach.

Nick took my car whenever I flew back home to be with my mom before she died. He stayed by my side as I re-acclimatized back on tour a month after her funeral. He gave me grace when my moods swung the pendulum. When the time came for us to split up, we remained friends even after he retired from caddying, and until he lost his battle with cancer.

Lonnie, a tall, lanky blonde, sauntered toward me in Belgium (the same summer I met Kenny). It was late Friday afternoon, and he was looking to work the weekend for a few extra bucks. Lonnie's laid-back personality both intrigued me and gave me pause. "I'll think about it and let you know," I told him.

I decided to say "yes," and I went on to finish second for the event (one of the European Tour events I played in 1994). Lonnie was a kind man, part of the veteran tour caddies on the LPGA. His disheveled appearance and laissez-faire attitude carried lightness and joy onto the course. Several years had passed since our Belgium weekend, but he was available for hire as a full-time caddy after Nick and I stopped working together.

Lonnie carried my bag, and me in some ways, into a second-place finish and my highest-ever payday during the week after the 9/11 terrorist attacks. Our two years together rode the ups and downs of tour life. Lonnie's personality was a good balance for my intensity and emotional tightness. My most memorable day of our time together was when I read a Scripture passage at his wedding. Every now and then, life on tour comes with more than just hitting a white ball into a small cup.

Just over a decade on tour had ticked away and Tat and I were closing out our second season together. She bore the brunt of my frustrations. I'd been reworking my golf swing, and it was a touch-and-go project. She held two of my most regrettable moments as a player and friend: one, when I broke a club over the top of my head during a tournament round, and two, when I slammed a club into the bag along with two of her fingers resting in the wrong place at the wrong time.

Her poise never changed, despite the hurt I caused. She remained faithful to working for me, but we decided to part ways after the last tournament of our second season together.

Who should I hire next? My career felt like it was closing out, but was I really *done*? Was it time to seriously consider retiring?

I didn't know Skyscraper (Jerry) very well. Standing at six-foot-seven, he towered over you like a skyscraper. I gave him a tryout in the first tournament of the 2008 season in Florida. He seemed like a nice enough guy and, as it turned out, he hit a high ten on the kindness scale. Skyscraper was a long-time caddy, and we worked well together. He was my guy for my fourteenth LPGA season.

I enjoyed Skyscraper; he was funny and positive with a lot of opinions. Usually, I allowed them to glance off me and kept walking. He adored me, and I really felt like he was rooting for me. My golf scores had been less than ideal. I was frustrated; the money list glared that I would be heading back to qualifying school at the end of the season. My status was a slow tumble downhill. Even so, loyal Skyscraper remained by my side each week, making sure I smiled regardless of my golf scores.

Caddy relationships hold the same rhythms as any other relationship, whether with a family member, friend, or spouse. Regardless of the ups and downs, I am grateful for each caddy that walked the fairways with me. God gave me the right person I needed most at opportune times.

91 // A NECESSARY ENDING

At the end of the 2008 LPGA season, I hung on the precipice of losing my playing status. Charley, my swing coach at the time, set up an introduction with a neuropsychologist to test my breathing efficiency and the electrical currents in my brain. I griped and moaned. *Why would I want to meet this doctor and spend* more *money?* Retirement felt imminent.

Fully unconvinced it was a good idea, I still agreed to meet with Dr. Royer—mostly to appease Charley. I didn't hide the chip on my shoulder when I shook Dr. Royer's hand. I remained pleasant but rigid. *Just get this over with so I can go on with my day,* I thought.

Twenty minutes later, I was putty in Dr. Royer's hands. My ego had to submit. I was faced with deficits that blared like strobe lights. My breathing was weak. The electricity in my brain raced 200 mile-per-hour hot laps around my neuronal highway. I was constantly in a fight-or-flight state. For the first time, I realized that there was a *physiological* reason for feeling like a mental and emotional breakdown was hiding just beyond the horizon. I started to feel compassion toward myself.

Despite having only one more event to play for the season, I agreed to try Dr. Royer's program—three months of breathing and neurofeedback training—and I would play the final stage of the LPGA Qualifying School Tournament to attempt to improve my playing status for the following year.

I trained hard by practicing my breathing several times a day. The breathing belt circled my stomach and my finger slid into the Pulse Sensor, a fingertip reader that measures the inter-beat intervals used to calculate heart rate variability (HRV). The devices were connected to the computer where I watched my breathing and HRV populate on the screen. I trained my diaphragm to breathe slower with more amplitude by blowing my belly up like a balloon and then squeezed all the air out on the exhale. This taught my lungs and heart to work together, called "cohesion."

First, I had to master cohesion sitting in a chair. Then, I transitioned to standing up. For the next level, to build cohesion under stress I walked up and down the yard holding the laptop with the cords attached to my body.

The final assignment took Dr. Royer and me to the golf course to practice maintaining this new breathing rhythm in my pre-shot routine and also during the walks between golf shots.

After a month of hard training, I put my new and refined breathing routine to the test at my last event of the season in Hawaii. Integrating the new rhythm immediately lowered my anxiety levels. Instead of being trapped by mechanical swing thoughts, my body felt released to do what I had trained it to do—freely swing.

After a first-round 69 that included a hole-in-one, I had a mediocre finish to the three-day event. My earnings were not enough and, for the first time in my career, I slipped outside the top 125 on the money list.

With only my LPGA Tour Class A status, the lowest priority status within the Tour membership, I returned to the Final Stage of qualifying school. I earned Class A status because I had been playing ten years on tour with more than ten tournaments each year.

It was a disaster. I played awful and missed the cut, not even close to making the final day of play. 2009 looked bleak. My Class A status might get me into one or two events, otherwise I had to try the Monday qualifiers—where only two players earn entry into that week's LPGA event based on an 18-hole score or move backwards and play on the Symetra Tour (the developmental tour of the LPGA at that time). Monday qualifiers are hard. I inevitably faced more failure. The pressure of the expectations pressed in on me like muddy water.

92 // BROKEN ENGAGEMENT

Nausea turned sleep against me. Tossing and turning to no avail, I laid awake, praying. I wanted things to be different, but my heart knew the truth. The next morning, I had to give the ring back.

I said yes to Cliff's marriage proposal in February 2008. On paper, Cliff and I seemed like a perfect pair. We both traveled for work, we shared mutual faith in Jesus, we enjoyed outdoor activities, we valued family, and we enjoyed home-improvement projects. But the hard things were hard. Honest communication was a major hurdle. We passive-aggressively buried our frustration and disappointment. Our unspoken expectations were left unattended. Silent resentment slinked its way into our daily phone calls.

In the fall of 2008, our counselors asked Cliff and me, "If you didn't get married in January, how would you feel?" We both shrugged.

Their raised eyebrows implied what we already knew but had not had the courage to admit—we needed to postpone the wedding. Our engagement was crumbling to pieces.

At the same time, as my golf performance was unraveling at a rapid rate, I was contemplating quitting for good.

My resentment for golf was heading towards hatred, and was ever-present at this point. Observers in my world were duped, believing I had it all. I had mastered the art of the façade. Behind my iron doors, however, I was miserable.

I hadn't made up my mind about breaking my engagement off until I was hitting golf balls after the first round at the first Symetra Tour event I played in March of 2009. Dr. Royer, who had come to caddy for me, stood next to my bag and gently suggested that Cliff and I were not honoring God's intention for marriage by stringing along our engagement with no purposeful plan in place. The Holy Spirit"s conviction rattled my entire being. Cliff was coming at the end of the tournament and I knew what I needed to do.

I tossed and turned. I felt nauseous and shaky.

As Cliff and I sat together on my couch at my condo, I sensed Cliff knew what was coming. Sadness filled the air as we walked through the conversation. Kindness and grace wrapped us in a blanket of comfort as we released our relationship together. I handed him the ring with tears streaming down my face. His grief looked back at me.

My life was falling apart. *What am I going to do now?*

93 // NAMING SEXUAL ABUSE

Amy, Dr. Royer's wife, was my online neurofeedback technician. She watched our sessions from her computer. When she adjusted the controls on my computer remotely, often from thousands of miles away, my brain and autonomic nervous system sorted the information, helping the electricity in my brain to slow down. Side conversations between Amy and me via the computer program's "chat room" sometimes distracted the sessions, but those moments were an important part of my process.

Amy's gentle curiosity and kindness invited my trust, and I slowly started opening up to her. In April, a month after ending my engagement to Cliff, Amy asked how I was feeling. After a few typed lines in the chat box, our conversation turned.

> *AMY: Do you feel like in your life that the high beta is hijacking your emotions? Like, if you look back at your dad and all the deaths of loved ones ... that it might have started creeping in and getting bigger?* [High beta are the fast-moving brain waves connected to your fight, flight, or freeze response.]
>
> *TRACY: I would say "yes," I have thought that. I'm sure my mom's death is a big part of me turning off some emotions.*
>
> *AMY: Can you think of times when you felt things really deeply? Maybe it felt almost too dangerous, so you took it down a notch to protect yourself from more pain?*
>
> *TRACY: After each death ... Yes, I can see that.*

The direction this conversation with Amy was heading unnerved me. But I also felt strangely compelled to keep going. I wanted—no, I *needed*—to say more. It had been bubbling up inside me and I couldn't keep stuffing it down anymore.

AMY: But I think that's where you crave that safe and comfortable place. You have those emotions, and you know you want to feel them, but you don't feel safe enough.

The struggle inside me raged. Did I dare share? I had only told a few people about my relationship with Coach.

TRACY: There was a bad relationship that definitely smashed my heart.

Sweat dripped down my back. Heat radiated off my skin. *What will Amy say?* I quickly messaged that I believed that for the most part I made good choices pleasing to God, but I had also made some really bad ones.

AMY: Why do you think you made bad ones?

TRACY: I think I was drawn to wanting to be loved for me, not for what I was good at.

AMY: Bingo! I think that is at the bottom of my mess, too.

Amy's vulnerability and genuine curiosity drew me to want to tell her about Coach. I still believed I had chosen to participate in the relationship, and I felt embarrassed.

TRACY: My awful experience when I was 17–18 years old led me down the wrong path even longer.

AMY: Did you think the wrong path would get your dad's attention? Like he might rescue you?

TRACY: He didn't know anything ... oblivious.

AMY: What about your mom—did she see anything?

TRACY: What happened was hidden, secret.

AMY: Come on, seriously? You were 17 and you experienced the biggest thing in your life, and they didn't know?

TRACY: I believe my mom knew something wasn't right—she confronted me once—but I said I was fine. We never talked about it again.

I told Amy I would share more when we were face to face. We completed my training session and set our next meeting for a few days later.

I felt raw, unsettled, a bit teetering on the edge of a precipice as I set up the laptop and Neurofeedback system on my coffee table at my condo in Florida. *How much more do I want to share?* The breathing belt was back on and the leads were attached to my head. The seconds ticked away as I waited for Amy to jump into our neurofeedback session from home in West Michigan. I attempted to distract myself by gazing out at the ocean that filled my horizon.

Ding! Amy's chat window opened on the screen. My heartbeat dropped to my stomach and a wave of electricity surged through my body.

If the opportunity presented itself, I planned to tell her what happened twenty years ago. I wanted her to know.

After a quick catch up, my heart rate quickened and I went for it. My fingers clicked out the words that had been ruminating in my mind.

TRACY: The bad relationship I had in high school was with a coach.

I shared that he was eight or nine years older and married. I back pedaled by making excuses and taking responsibility. *What would Amy do with me? What would she think? How would she respond?* Seconds passed that felt like minutes.

AMY: Tracy, that was sexual abuse. This makes me so angry, and I am so sorry.

I stared at the screen, fixated on those two little words.
Really? Sexual abuse? I sat frozen in front of the keyboard.

94 // AN END AT CORNING

I pulled out of the driveway for the eleven-hour drive ahead. New Rochelle, New York, was my final destination—my first LPGA Tour Monday qualifier in fifteen years.

I played two Symetra Tour events in March 2009 and both were horrific. My attention sprayed everywhere except down the fairways, where it belonged. Adding salt to my wound of having only Class A status on the LPGA Tour, I missed both cuts.

As the miles clicked by, my resolve thickened. I would give one hundred percent of myself on Monday and play all my cards. After the qualifier, Dr. Royer would be onsite and, together, we'd do our first breathing and brain assessments with several LPGA Tour players. We hoped to intrigue a few players to train with Dr. Royer's program and build traction among professional golfers. Silently, I wondered if it would be an avenue to walk away from competitive golf.

If I could par the eighteenth hole, I might have a chance. The course was playing hard, but my competitive nature rose to the occasion. I signed for an even par 72 and waited with the other dozen players to finish for the final results.

I tied for second. But with only two spots available, a playoff would decide which one of us received the second qualifying spot. I bogeyed the first playoff hole, while the other player made par. I would not get into the tournament.

I packed my disappointment away for not qualifying and turned my attention to working with Dr. Royer the next day, Tuesday.

Dr. Royer's optimism was contagious. A few players showed interest in the neurofeedback program, on which I would be the point person and technician. Excitement for the opportunity collided with my performance anxiety. What if I messed it up and didn't handle the program well? I will be working with my peers, and I didn't want to look stupid.

After wrapping up our assessment, I headed back to Michigan. A little more than halfway back, my phone rang. A Daytona Beach number flashed on the screen. Curious and perplexed, I answered it.

"What?" I said in disbelief to the voice on the other end. "I'm now in the tournament? I'm closer to Michigan than New York. I can't get back there in time to tee it up tomorrow."

The LPGA Tour had made a mistake. The low qualifier got into the field off the priority list. The two of us who had tied for second should have been given entry into the tournament. Owning their mistake, the tour offered me a spot in the following week's event in Corning, New York. *Ugh.*

"Okay, I'll figure out a way to get there. Thank you for the opportunity." I clenched my jaw in response.

I had only played the Corning event a few times during my career. It usually landed on a good week to take a break in my schedule. I hired one of my former caddies and prepped like I had a hundred times before.

With only a few competitive rounds under my belt for the year, my first-round 71 surprised me. Day two was a different story, the wheels came apart and I crashed and burned with a 78. An unfamiliar apathy fell over me. I wasn't angry or disappointed—just numb.

Stuck in Corning until my flight on Sunday, I joined some other players for a pick-up basketball game on Saturday. I meandered the day away, excited to get back to Michigan for a quick turnaround before leaving for a biblical study trip to Egypt, Jordan, and Israel. It would be my third trip to the Middle East, but my first to Egypt.

Before touching down in Michigan on Sunday, I *knew*. My heart was no longer invested in stringing along my golf career. I might even have hated the game at this point if I am being truly honest.

Clarity hit me: I had just played my last competitive rounds on the LPGA Tour. I was done. I didn't make a big announcement. I silently left the tour behind. I wondered if anyone would notice my absence.

95 // FRONT ROW AGAIN

It's our fifth family funeral in twelve years, four of which occurred during a span of six years of my professional golf career. While Dad's lung cancer progressed with vengeance, it was pneumonia that seized his weak lungs. I loved my dad, and yet the absence of any emotional relationship with him left me in a pool of shallow grief.

A familiar exhaustion weighed heavy on me as I sat in the front row of the funeral home that December day in 2010. Seven days earlier, I was watching over my sister's kids so that she and my brother-in-law, Rich, could visit my dad. Within an hour of their arrival, Dad had slipped into a coma and I received the first of two calls from my sister, Debbie.

I went into a state of shock. We knew he wasn't doing well, but we thought he had more time. I had a trip planned for the following month to go see him. My mind was spinning in confusion.

When she placed the receiver to my father's ear, I said, "Dad, I love you." A lump grew in my throat. "It's okay. You can let go. We'll be okay." My voice cracked and tears finally came. I don't know if he heard me. I hope he did.

I went back to playing with my nieces and nephew. But my mind was in Idaho. A few hours later, I got the second call and Debbie said, "Dad is gone."

The kids were already asleep as questions swept through my mind. *How was I going to tell my nieces and nephew that their grandfather had died? Should they come with me out to the funeral?* I folded the laundry and cried.

I finalized the first wave of arrangements. The kids absorbed the news as best they could for their ages and my sister, Rich, and I decided it best for them to stay with friends and I would fly to Idaho on my own. Once I arrived, my sister and I faced one battle after another. Grieving would have to wait.

I shook myself back to reality, to that front-row seat. No one else in the family wanted to speak. I said "yes," even though it was the last thing I wanted to do. *I didn't want to disappoint anyone, and I knew how to shut down and handle hard things, as usual.* One last time, I played the role of Dad's trophy to an overpacked room who loved Tom Hanson. Unknowingly at the time, seven months in the future I would begin to name the ways in which he missed my heart. But, at that moment I did my best to honor the man who gave me life.

Once again, I faced the dreaded receiving line. My plastic smile never changed even as I nodded at each person and shook their hand. I glanced down the line to see when it would be over.

My internal alarm system screamed. I yanked myself back in line, away from Coach's stare. I glanced across the room to where friends stood, silently pleading for help. No one understood. I froze, unable to move—surrounded by people and yet totally alone.

Tight and controlled, I extended him an obligatory side hug and spun to the next person as quickly as I could. Thankfully, he disappeared and I didn't see Coach again.

It had been several years since I wrote a letter to Coach stating I wanted no relationship with him: "We are not friends. Please let me live my life." He had indeed left me alone, for the most part. Until he showed up at Dad's funeral. Once again, I had to hide the story in the recesses of my soul.

The lie was pulling me back into the shadows.

96 // A NEW ROUTINE

A shadow fell over my left shoulder. "Tracy, can you help me with the computer again?" I hid my eyeroll.

"Sure, Kay. How can I help?"

In the last few months, my transition to working at Neurocore as a brain assessment specialist and technician had been enlightening. Technically, I still resided in Florida where I maintained my condo; however, since I had co-ownership in a house and Dr. Royer gave me a job, I chose to rest and recover from tour life in West Michigan.

My new "business casual" wardrobe was more "athletic business casual." Going into an office, working a set schedule, interfacing with clients, and leaving work behind at the end of the day demanded quite the learning curve. At least I was having fun.

My job at Neurocore gave me much-needed flexibility. If I wanted to take two weeks off to facilitate a trip to the lands of the Bible, I could. I didn't have to work on Christmas Day; I always took time to see my sister over the holidays.

I realized this was not a *real* work scenario, but it became my new normal.

Kay handled Neurocore's Quality Control. She mostly worked from home on the phone, but she had been coming into the office more frequently to help with the brain assessments. Kay was exceptional at invading my personal space—not something on which I was keen. Her kindness and soft voice always seemed to weaken my resolve, however. I even started gravitating towards her when I saw her in the office.

Life after golf continued quietly. I averaged five rounds a summer for the first three years after quitting the tour. The majority of those rounds were pro-am charity events and came with a paycheck. I didn't miss my past life at all and avoided talking about golf as much as possible.

My new office routine wore off soon enough, though I enjoyed my co-workers.

I typically drove the thirty minutes to work in silence, but occasionally I flipped the radio on for some company. One particular day, Moody Radio caught my attention. The guests, Milan and Kay Yerkovich, were having a conversation about their book, *How We Love*.

In the wake of my dad's passing and heartache from another failed relationship, I felt lonely, empty, and like a failure. Milan Yerkovich's voice reached through the radio and grabbed my soul. I don't remember the exact words, but it was something like, "When we have experienced many losses, our heart begins to believe it is not worth to love at all."

His words pierced me and made me begin to think. I was depleted. I started to realize how loss in my life had piled up. The lack of emotional engagement from my parents; the years of Coach's "grooming" (building a false relationship so as to use me sexually); two broken engagements and many failed romances; and five family deaths due to cancer—*why would I want to risk love?*

Back at Neurocore, Kay's intuition latched onto me. She knew I held a Christian faith, but sensed my guarded heart.

"Would you be interested in doing a Bible study over the winter, Tracy?"

Kay's sincerity drew me in. "Yes, that sounds good," I replied.

Besides seeing Kay at work, I drove to Norton Shores, Michigan, every week or every other week, as my schedule allowed, to watch a video Bible study together. The study focused on one key verse, Galatians 2:20:

"I have been crucified with Christ. It is no longer I who live, but Christ who lives in me. And the life I now live in the flesh I live by faith in the Son of God, who loved me and gave Himself for me."

I had read Galatians 2:20 many times, but did I really believe it to be true for me?

We worked our way through the book of Romans, focusing on chapters 6, 7, and 8. As we traveled through the study, Kay helped me sort through the truth: *If I really believe that Jesus is who He says He is, what does that mean for my life?*

Those three chapters in Romans took me on a journey. Romans 6 challenged me to recognize and be more honest about how I had chased love and acceptance through my performance my whole life. I could *choose* rest (something I'm still working on). Chapter 7 challenged me to consider the patterns behind my struggles. Chapter 8 was the cliffhanger: *Who am I, really?* For the first time, I started wrestling with God in deep and profound ways. A process that is still unfolding even today.

During these months of Bible study with Kay, I returned to the Middle East. On our visit to Jordan, I stood on the bank of the Jabbok River. The story of Jacob came to life; somewhere along that river, Jacob wrestled with the Angel of the Lord all night (Genesis 32:22–32). The bank of my own wrestling with God took me into a renewed relationship with Him that I had not known previously. In a small way it felt like a new beginning.

As we neared the end of the Bible study, one thing still plagued me.

"What about Coach?" I asked Kay. *What should I do with that?*

Kay realized I needed someone to help me process my high school trauma before I could allow myself to fully grab hold of God's unconditional love through His Son, Jesus.

Looking back, I can see how God's unfolding plan for my healing started with Tim and Amy Royer and continued through Kay. Then it landed me with another Tracy: Tracy Johnson, a kind, fierce woman who would walk with me into the valleys of the shadow of death and pain of my past trauma, and help me to climb out on the other side.

Dad and Mom celebrated with me over the 1994 Christmas season after I earned my LPGA Tour Card.

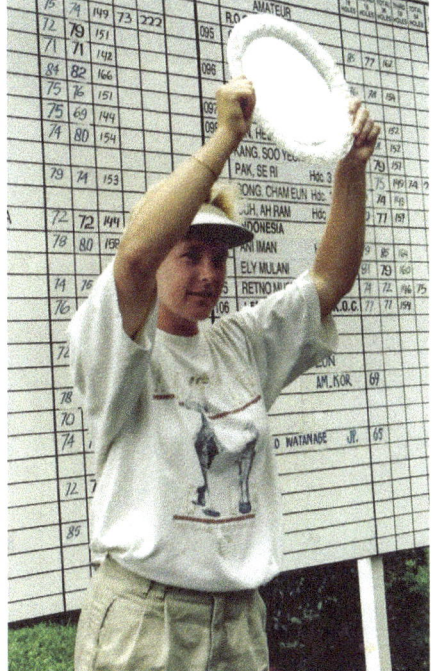

In my first year as a pro I won the 1994 Ladies Indonesian Open, the third of four tournaments on the Ladies Asian Tour from Thailand to Malaysia to Indonesia to Taiwan.

Visiting the one and only Randy Henry, my childhood golf instructor who was my biggest encouragement throughout my career.

My beautiful mom, Marcella Hanson, at age 50.

May 1998, less than two weeks before our brave mother lost her battle with melanoma cancer.

My nieces Haley and Courtney and nephew André in 2005. They have their Aunt Tracy wrapped around their every wish.

Three sisters: Me, Debbie, and Sheli, 2000.

PART FIVE:
THE HEALING

97 // THE BLINK OF AN EYE

Panic rippled through my body. White-knuckled, I gripped the steering wheel. "Exit left," the GPS voice boomed out of the phone. I obeyed. My first counseling appointment with Tracy Johnson was waiting in downtown Kalamazoo ten minutes away. *What am I getting myself into?*

I circled the one-way streets for the third time, no closer to knowing where I should park. The 90-degree summer heat radiated through the car windows. Should I park on the street or behind the building where permits are required? Is there free parking since it's Saturday? My thoughts ricocheted in my mind. *What am I doing here?*

I pulled on the door, but it didn't budge. *I think this is the correct building.* I peered into the locked entryway, but my efforts proved fruitless.

See, I should climb right back into my car and go home, my inner voice stated matter-of-factly.

I paced the sidewalk, my mind clouded with questions. *Why don't I have Tracy's cell phone number?*

Just as I turned away from the entry door, a voice from behind startled me out of my trance. "Tracy, I'm so sorry this door was locked, I forgot it was Saturday and I was looking for you at the door in the back of the building. You're in the right place. Let's go up to my office."

My polite smile covered my fright as sweat slithered down my back. The hit of cold indoor air jolted me back to awareness. No going back now.

I sat in my rigid, upright upholstered chair like a statue while Tracy Johnson rocked casually in her office chair a few feet across from me. Her smile eased my discomfort, slightly. Words seemed to have escaped my brain—all I did was stare back and hope something happened.

Internally, a war raged. *Where should I start? What if I don't do it right? I want counseling to help, but maybe I'm making this into a much bigger deal than it actually is.*

Before I knew it I was clutching the steering wheel and navigating my way to the freeway for the hour-plus drive home. Time had stood still in her office. If I hadn't written down the questions Tracy asked me to think about for our next appointment two weeks later, I would have no recollection of what happened during our ninety minutes.

What keeps me from being fully alive "here"?
Where am I taking up too much space in my life?
Where am I taking up the appropriate amount of space?
When did I stop dreaming?
Where did I start losing myself?

My head was spinning. I thought Tracy and I were going to talk about the abuse, not all this other stuff. She asked a lot of questions about my parents. Other than some frustrations and annoyances, I'd always believed I had a good childhood. Tracy's questions really made me begin to wonder.

98 // NAMING TRUTH

Scavenging through my childhood was disheartening. Naming the emotional neglect from my parents felt unfair since they weren't around to ask them questions and get their side of it. Yet, it was true. My basic needs were always met, sure. I had an abundance of opportunities to participate in sports; we had a nice house and lived a good middle-class existence. But so much more was absent.

I wasn't nurtured or encouraged to express my feelings. Those words that I penned in my journal stared back at me, detailing a harsh reality. *My femininity was squashed, and I believed being a tomboy was my only option. I have lived my life covered with shame.* How much of my life have I lost because of self-contempt—believing that I was the problem?

Tracy Johnson handed me a laminated page filled with words. I was instantly transported back to my third-grade speech therapy—it looked just like a vocabulary quiz. The cool sheet of words in my hands matched my emotional freeze. *Am I incapable of feeling?* Tracy was working hard to draw me out.

"Soul deadness," Tracy explained, "is when a heart is dulled to its own pain. This list of emotional descriptive words will help you find your own words."

As my bimonthly appointments that summer and fall came and went, I came more and more undone. It was like ripping a piece of duct tape off my bare skin—the sting was abrupt and lingered. In psychology speak, I entered the state of disintegration. I didn't like any of it, but I chose to trust the process.

I knew my relationship with my dad was filled with disappointments. With each passing session, I started to understand just how hard I had performed for his love and adoration. I realized growing up in an emotional desert left me emotionally undernourished and vulnerable. Going to counseling is not an exercise of blaming others for our pain or heartaches. The work is to name what is true and the impact on our hearts, minds, and souls. For more than three decades, I mastered the art of hiding. Despite my success, I still believed I wasn't enough—that I was broken at the core.

I gazed at a picture of my seventeen-year-old face on the night of my high school graduation. My vacant eyes stared back. For the first time I saw an empty, lonely girl desiring to be loved and cared for. I was navigating my whole world, alone. How did I manage finishing high school, playing a full summer golf schedule, prepping to move to college—all while carrying the burden of a secret sexual relationship that wasn't really a relationship?

Ironically, the consequence of "hustling for my worthiness," as Dr. Brené Brown describes, is a false sense of love that only adds to the inability to open myself to be fully loved and known. In turn, I didn't have the ability to fully love, either.

Tracy's compassion and empathy frightened me, but also pressed in upon me. My resolve weakened. After a moment of uncomfortable silence, her sudden movement toward me jolted me upright. Leaning in, her knees mere millimeters from mine, my counselor's eyes glistened.

"Tracy, IT WAS NOT YOUR FAULT."

Her fierceness shot an arrow right into my heart. Heat and energy flushed through my chest. For the second time in Tracy's presence, tears streamed down my face.

"It was not my fault" squeaked out of my mouth.

The truth stared back at me. *I am a survivor of childhood sexual abuse.*

I had no idea how I would travel to the other side of that daunting mountain, but in that moment I reached a new precipice on my journey of healing.

99 // A YEAR OF GROWTH

"I think it's time for you to consider where golf fits in your life again," Tracy's words were soft but strong.

"Wait a second," I replied, "a year ago you said that you were *glad* I didn't play golf anymore. Now you're saying the opposite?" I threw my hands in the air.

Tracy laughed. "Yes, that is what I'm saying."

I collapsed into my chair. Seconds passed before I broke the silence between us. "I don't understand."

For twelve months, I had rummaged through the hidden rooms of my heart, naming hard truths. It was quite a list.

My childhood was void of emotional nurturing.

My tomboy persona was one-dimensional, preventing nourishment to my femininity. I held judgment and contempt over that little girl my entire life.

My dad paraded me around like a trophy; humiliation followed me in his footsteps. His issues with pornography violated my innocence.

My mom's undiagnosed depression and silent suffering left me adrift.

I was sexually abused.

Tracy laid out the task in front of me: *Walk into her husband Mark's office, extend a handshake, and tell him who I am.* Heat and blood flooded my face and my heart pounded. "Really?" Her snicker confirmed any doubt.

I walked my trembling body down the hall and crossed the threshold into Mark's office. As I reached out my hand, Mark stood up from behind his desk looking a bit confused.

"Hi, my name is Tracy Hanson. I'm an LPGA Tour Professional and I'm kind of a big deal." A nervous laugh tumbled out of me.

Mark played along perfectly. I walked out of his office with a newfound bounce of confidence. Golf didn't immediately return as a trusted friend, but the possibility that my story with golf was not stuck at a dead end did. It was time to embrace the reality that golf (and generally, sports) could simultaneously hold both harm and blessing in my life.

100 // GROUP WORK

I entered the room for our first group meeting feeling hopeful and nervous. The seven other people in our mixed-gender group had already nestled into their spots. A year ago, at my first group experience in the fall of 2012, I had left disappointed. This time around, I hoped the additional year of counseling and added confidence would help me be more vulnerable and take advantage of the sessions. My desire was to dig deeper and risk more.

For our first task, we traced our actual body outline on a long piece of butcher paper. The act of being traced didn't bother me, but, after taping my paper on the wall, I stared blankly at my cartoon-shaped body. *How will this come to life over the next five days?* My insides tightened as I wondered.

My group mates were kind in their pursuit of me and my story. "How would you like to represent your loneliness on your outline?" one inquired.

Turning toward the paper, I drew a line around my entire torso. The weight of how alone and empty I have felt for so long pressed into me.

The next question caught me off guard as well. "What is your relationship with sport?"

My hand drew two blocks on the outline of my shoulders. I labeled one "Performance" and the other "Succeed." I knew my dad's pride was tightly wound around my golf. A couple years before, when I retired from the LPGA Tour, I was so nervous to tell my dad I was done.

The next thing I drew on my body outline was a small bubble near my broken heart with the words "Joy" and "Fun" inside. I added a heart broken in five pieces near where my real heart would be on the body outline. Each piece held a description. Broken heart. Shattered. Crushed. Destroyed. Smashed. For the first time in my life, the bind of ambivalence in my story became real. I tried hard to live in a black or white world, but the truth is that while much harm had been done to me, the sport had brought many good things to my life too.

"Would you be open to a role-play?" our group supervisor asked.

My mouth went dry. "Uh, maybe. I guess so," I replied.

The role-play exercise was to speak words I wanted and needed to say to my dad. One of my male group members agreed to sit in as my dad. I sat across from him numb and emotionally flat. Words and emotions whispered out of me, but the appropriate strength and volume I needed to voice my pain remained lodged in my throat. It was so hard to name—more honestly—my anger, sadness, and pain towards my dad.

It wasn't until I was alone later with my journal that I finally let the words tumble onto the page.

Dad, you failed me. You stomped on my beauty. You did not teach me to care and respect myself. You objectified me, were passive and not protective, and I didn't feel safe. You betrayed our family. We needed you but you chose your beer, smoking, pub friends, and infidelity. I wanted and needed you to love me for who I am, not what I did. Your pornography shattered my mind and heart. I hated the way you treated Mom. You didn't make our home a safe place. I hate you and somehow I still love you.

Even as the truth of my story unfolded on my butcher paper, and with the help of the role-play, I struggled to believe the depth of harm evident in my story. I needed my group members to mirror the pain, sorrow, and sadness back to me. As they did, my heart slowly began to grieve.

I was exhausted, but not ready for the week to be over. With each passing session, I felt safer and more comfortable. My story was welcomed without judgment. My groupmates pursued my heart with curiosity, fierceness, truth, and kindness. And God pursued my heart through them.

There were two last things I needed to do.

The opportunity to be baptized in Lake Michigan was available for all participants on our last day. I had wondered all week if I would wade into the cold October water. I didn't want to do it to feel included or because it was expected. I didn't need to be baptized to publicly declare my faith as a follower of Jesus, I had already done that years before.

What I needed to consider was a declaration of war against the enemy of my soul.

Would I choose to give God full access to my entire story, the pain, the shame, and all of the ugly parts? What kept burning in my gut was that I needed to bury my disdain for my femininity in the dark waters and resurface declaring my beauty. Not a physical beauty, but that I am fearfully and wonderfully made by my Creator.

My first step into the crisp water jolted my nerve endings. I reached out to Mark Johnson and Chris Stark, who had become men I trusted. Their smiles encouraged me forward. Together they laid me back into the water and I felt the love of Jesus hug me as I was pulled up into the fresh air.

Being more vulnerable and honest about my story with my group was excruciatingly hard, but so life-giving at the same time. Later that night, as all the groups gathered together, I laughed. I danced. I celebrated another step in my healing journey.

101 // ALONE AGAIN

My thoughts left me in a heap of angst. *I moved to Michigan after leaving the LPGA Tour for community, but now everything is changing again.*

My three years of living full-time in one location with a somewhat normal routine allowed me time to rest and recover from my life on Tour. I had developed new friendships and started counseling too. But now, change was coming, and change was not easy for me

Now what? Do I stay? What am I supposed to be doing? Who am I?

My work with Neurocore had offered some travel opportunities to Orlando to work with the Orlando Magic basketball team. It wasn't going to be a forever job, but it gave me a temporary purpose and an outlet for my growing restlessness. Travel, embedded in my DNA after living almost two decades on the road, whisked me away from the mundane office work. Furthermore, I was learning that I can't stay tied to people just to make me feel okay about myself.

I have my own wings and I need to exercise them.

Fear lingered close to the surface most days, though. In the shadows of post-tour life, I felt small and insignificant. Tracy Johnson continued to help me pursue truth in our counseling sessions. One of the truths was that I *do* have something to offer. The growing energy inside me didn't want to live small anymore—even if that meant facing hard changes. God was preparing something new for me. Whatever it was just felt really ambiguous.

When I started counseling, getting in touch with my feelings was like staring into a dense fog. I heavily leaned on the laminated *Feeling Words* chart Tracy had given me. Still today, more than a decade later, acknowledging my feelings to myself and others feels risky and often messy. I still stumble at times trying to find the right words that reflect my emotions. Sometimes it takes time to formulate my thoughts, and I often have to retract my first attempts and try again. But my emotional muscles continue to grow stronger.

Thankfully, for the most part, I am expanding emotionally in a positive way. I value myself and I make decisions without feeling guilty or worrying about disappointing others. I am thankful for the people in my life who welcome my feelings with kindness, who have encouraged me along my journey, and who also challenge me when I regress.

I *do* matter.

For over two decades, golf controlled my life. Every time I pushed the tee into the ground, I attached my self-worth to my results; the wave of shame crashed hard with every failure.

Playing professional golf also required a high level of selfishness. It's more than a full-time job-plus-travel—it's an entire existence. I often struggled with feeling like I didn't belong, except among my sister and her family, and I hustled for connection by overextending myself to people. Codependency (managing other people's feelings *for them* through my behavior) slinked its way into my psyche, nurtured by my trauma. I led an exhausting existence where nothing was ever enough. I lived from a posture that *I am never enough.*

As I have returned to competitive golf as a senior tour player, I am growing in not allowing my performance results to have the final say. I now believe that my longings for connection and belonging are good and do matter. I embraced the hard changes as they unfolded and have experienced goodness in my relationships, in being content, in pursuing what God has opened up before me. I am going to be okay.

102 // KENYA

"I'll go," I finally answered Tim, my friend at Athletes in Action. He had been encouraging me to go on the 2013 AIA golf ministry trip to Kenya for months.

I felt inadequate on two fronts: I hadn't been playing much golf and I would need to show up well as one of the professional golfers from the United States and the only female golfer on the trip. And a mission trip had never been high on my priority list. I couldn't deny the timing, however. My curiosity stirred with the possibility that golf and ministry can go hand in hand.

I laughed when Eric, our leader, asked a couple weeks before we were to depart if I would lead one of our morning devotionals on the topic of identity. A love/hate relationship with the word "identity" lived inside me. What does it really mean to have an identity in Jesus? Leading a group of people I hardly knew in devotional teaching felt daunting. I liked blending into the background, not being the one front and center. To share about identity made me quiver because I felt like I was still wrestling with what it means. It's one thing to say my identity is in Jesus, it's another thing to break free from surviving, and thriving, from a performance acceptance identity most of my life.

As our team sat in our circle, still jet-lagged, I intermingled 1 Kings 18:18–20 with my personal story. Elijah, one of God's prophets, went head-to-head with the prophets of Baal on top of Mount Carmel. God's people were stuck between two opinions: Should they worship the idol Baal for its provision or turn back and trust God? God would go on to prove His point by destroying all 450 prophets of Baal, but God never forces His people (us) to follow Him. It was their choice, as it is also ours.

"I have not made trouble for Israel," Elijah replied. "But you and your father's family have. You have abandoned the Lord's commands and have followed the Baals. Now summon the people from all over Israel to meet me on Mount Carmel. And bring the four hundred and fifty prophets of Baal and the four hundred prophets of Asherah, who eat at Jezebel's table." So Ahab sent word throughout all Israel and assembled the prophets on Mount Carmel." (1 Kings 18:18–20 NIV)

Ahab called Elijah "troubler of Israel." But Elijah refused this false identity and remained calm and confident in what the LORD had asked him to do. A fascinating component of the story lies in Elijah's name which means: "The Lord is my God." Elijah's identity was in the Lord, and he lived it out right there on top of Mount Carmel. I challenged our group that we also have access to this same identity—*the Lord is my God.*

For over two decades I wavered—and still struggle today—between two opinions. My identity is professional golf; my identity is in the Lord as my God. Golf won the battle most days during my playing career, leaving me feeling empty and lost even in the midst of success. I believe we are to pursue excellence in whatever we do—whether sports, business, or the arts—but what if what we do is laced with stress and anxiety? In that case, we are bound in the chains of hustling for our worth through performance.

I challenged our group—a personal challenge as well—to see that we could enjoy golf and the desire to perform well, but live out the gospel story to change our identity. Instead of looking toward empty idols (a golf score, money, status, etc.) for our worth, we can turn our face toward the living God who loves us for who we are, not for what we do.

Kenya captured my heart. Words fail to describe the beauty and intrigue of the land and wildlife along the southern end of the Rift Valley. The people had grit. Hardship was wrapped with joy. Laughter and play rose above circumstances.

Poverty, vacant eyes, and filth walked me through the Soweto slums in Nairobi, Kenya; leaving me heartbroken and speechless. My world and theirs were two sides of a wide chasm. Yet, sport and play were universal languages that bound our humanity together.

The best souvenir I carried home from the trip was the time I spent with the nine young adult men in our group. They charmed and enlightened me. Instead of keeping them at a distance, I opened myself up to them just as they opened themselves up to me. Their kindness, curiosity, and vulnerability invited my own vulnerability. They welcomed me to speak truth into their lives. They gave me the gift and taste of an authentic relationship.

I came home with a little more assurance that *the Lord is my God*.

103 // RECOVERY WEEK

Tension crept across my chest. "We don't care what you do, but you have to *all* do it together," the instructor said. I scanned the other faces in the room, unease undoubtedly showing in my own expression.

It was Monday, the evening of our first full day at The Allender Center Recovery Week in the spring of 2014. We were given a movie to watch, which meant I didn't have to talk to anyone. Honestly, I just wanted to hide away in my room. I would do my part, sit, and observe—no more. I came to Recovery Week for myself, after all, not to engage in group activities with nine other women.

The retreat center rested on a hillside overlooking the magical Hood Canal in Washington State. The Olympic Mountain range stood at attention in the distance under wispy clouds smearing a brilliant blue sky. Recovery Week is a five-day group counseling experience for childhood sexual abuse survivors. I still struggled accepting the label of "survivor," but it's true—*I am a survivor*.

I wanted help connecting my feelings to the facts of my sexual abuse story. I was a pro at being emotionally flat and numb when telling my story. During one of the early group teaching times, I scribbled, "Numbing is a by-product of judgment." For all the good work I had been doing in counseling, I continued to handcuff myself in contempt for what had happened to me.

The ambivalence of sexual abuse (where a person is violated and simultaneously experiences arousal) is a source of deepest shame. Holding judgment and shame against myself felt easier than naming the truth of betrayal, or grieving that my innocence was lost at a young age, or honoring and blessing my longings and desires as *good*. Owning that my body holds beauty twisted my gut into knots of discomfort. As I moved through each session, a loud echo rang in my head: *Where am I not telling my story more honestly?*

On the second night, the group decided to trek down to a nearby hotel bar for our activity. Our options were slim, and we wanted a break from the retreat center. Our group took over several small tables, squishing them together. I wasn't a big drinker, but I accepted a glass of wine. My self-critic jabbered inside my head. *I am way outside of my comfort zone. What can I offer? I don't belong at the table with these women.* I sat quietly, listening to and observing the laughter and stories. The expansive windows streamed in the last of the evening light. Slowly, ever so slowly, my body began to relax.

On the third evening, the leaders shared an unusual group assignment. We were each handed a $20 bill. The van would drop us off downtown of Union—if you can call it a downtown. We were tasked with shopping for "a gift from Jesus," something that reflected our time at the retreat and our story. *Ugh—I hate shopping.* By the time we stumbled out of the van, we had just forty-five minutes before our dinner reservation which, again, would be just the ten of us.

I attached myself to a couple other gals and followed them in and out of one artsy shop and the next. As time ticked away, I remained empty handed, not finding anything to fit my taste and meeting the assignment. Panic moved full force within me. *I am going to fail the task: my worst nightmare.*

In the final ten minutes before dinner, I walked into one more small shop covered wall to wall with pictures, books, and figurines. Nothing of interest—or so I thought. I scaled the spiral staircase in the back corner and another large, cluttered space smacked me in the face. I turned to the right and froze.

In the back corner, upstairs, on a bottom shelf, of this final stop, I saw it. Heat flushed my cheeks and a tear welled. *This is it.*

The frame, separated into four sections and was united in the middle with a small mirror. Each quadrant had pictures of female images in wispy dresses with four distinct words in script on a mauve-colored background: *Beautiful, Dream, Explore, Create.*

Jesus sees me. He invited me to see my face and beauty in the mirror. He implored me to consider: Will I dream, explore, and create? Shaking, I showed my purchase to two of the ladies. They burst into wide smiles and smothered me in hugs.

Our table was lively with chatter at the restaurant. My glass of wine nudged my courage as I smiled and giggled with the other women. The table noise quieted, and I felt several pairs of eyes turn towards me.

Swallowing my discomfort, I started to share how I had believed my entire adult life that I don't belong at the table of women. I'm not a wife or a mother. I don't feel *womanly*. As soon as the words left my lips, the kindness of the group enveloped me.

"Tracy, I love it when you smile."

"You are a joy to be with."

"We love being with you."

Heads nodded in agreement. My face fell in embarrassment. More words filled the air, pronouncing just how much everyone was enjoying my presence. I couldn't help but lift my head and smile.

Those three nights pushed me to consider that I do belong and am welcomed at the table of women.

104 // NEW KIND OF TRAINING

My wheels squealed to a halt ten minutes late to my first day of Narrative-Focused Trauma Care Training with The Allender Center in Chicago. It had been nearly four months since I completed Recovery Week. The ease of my self-hatred rattled my core as I parked and rushed into the Embassy Suites. *I hate being late.* My heart thumped, threatening to beat out of my chest, and I barely felt my feet on the floor as I darted toward the conference room. I should have arrived the night before—what a terrible decision to drive through morning traffic in the Windy City.

Pausing at the door, I inhaled deeply then exhaled. *You can do this, Tracy.* The slap of humiliation hit me as I pushed the door open, catching a few eyes glancing my way. Ducking low, I made a beeline for an open seat in the back of the packed ballroom. Thankfully, Dr. Allender was still making introductions. *You're here. Breathe. It's going to be okay.* With my notebook open and pen in hand, I settled in for our first teaching.

I had approached my counseling journey much like my golf career, relying on self-discipline, hard work, and a general hope that I could figure things out along the way. Even today, that vein of performance and perfectionism slithers its way into most things I do. Success has followed, even beyond my natural capabilities, but the kickback to striving for perfection is utter exhaustion. Reality check: Perfection is unattainable.

I took one step at a time along my journey. Individual counseling with Tracy Johnson—check. Small group experiences where sharing stories in community drew out vulnerability with more honesty—check. The Narrative-Focused Trauma Care Training with The Allender Center was my next big step to lead me toward my next chapter: becoming a Lay Counselor.

Life is full of surprises.

Over the next six months of 2014-2015, we met four times for four days of teaching and small group experience. We had reading and writing assignments before each session. Each writing assignment topic needed to be written from a ground-level perspective with as many details as we remembered, including people, smells, sounds, colors, textures, locations, and emotions. While it *sounded* easy, it certainly was not. As people, we tend to share or write about our lives from a ten-thousand-foot view, sometimes even higher. A few clicks of the keyboard brings a smidge of honesty, but we mostly hover around what sounds good and makes us feel good.

In each weekend session of our training, we read our story aloud to our group and facilitator, and then all were given permission to further pursue aspects of the story for thirty minutes. There is a short list of rules around engagement, but it rarely feels good to be in the hot seat. Sometimes, questions land in a dead end. Or one curious question sneaks through a small crack in the story and breaks all hell loose.

There is beauty in narrative work within a group setting. Where I am blind as the storyteller, others bear witness to the gaps in my storytelling. When curiosity collides with honoring our stories, we come out of hiding and more accurate truth turns us to the light. I won't lie, it can be painful, often maddening, but it also bears the fruit of healing. In the crossroads of remembering and naming the harm we each experienced, God brought beauty out of ashes, hope emerged from darkness, and we tasted the purpose for which we were created.

We all left these weekends exhausted. The teachings came at us like water from a fire hose. So much to learn and digest. I tried to walk into each small group session open and ready to move deeper into the crevices of my story, yet, when it was my time to read, an inner battle of locking the shutters tightly and keeping the darkness inside ensued.

My curiosity skills strengthened with each story I heard from other group members. I learned the art of attunement, kindness, and truth-telling. As a fellow friend said about story narrative work: "These skills are caught, not taught."

Throughout our first three weekends together, my small group experienced a roller coaster of emotions. We erupted in anger, resulting in one individual storming out of the room. We cried together. We navigated conflict and disagreement. And, above all, we came to honor and hold each story with awe and reverence.

Our fourth and final weekend was a little different. We explored what possibilities might emerge for the future as a result of the narratives of our lived experiences. When I first saw the assignment for session four, I had trouble imagining what might happen, but I was hopeful.

105 // COAT OF ARMS

I read the assignment for a fifth time. I was to create a personal "Coat of Arms" for my calling in the Kingdom of God. I wanted to slink away as the negative thoughts ran rampant through my mind: *You don't have a calling. You're going to fail. You're not enough. You're unlovable, so why even try?*

Creating art with the stroke of a pencil has never been my gift. I color *inside* established lines. Lines represent rules. Rules create *containment.* Containment keeps me together. As a professional golfer, I had to learn to contain my emotions, to aim for stoicism. Darkness contained my story of trauma for decades and supported my striving for perfection.

Containment helped me survive.

But if containment lacks relief, it becomes an emotion-eating parasite. Thankfully, I had found relief through counseling with Tracy and through Lay Counseling training with The Allender Center. Containment can be a blessing in certain situations, but it can also be a thorn in my side. I'm not sure I'll ever fully rid myself of the tendencies, but I am more capable of noticing when I try to contain my shame or emotions out of self-protection. I can pluck out the parasite sooner. I also am growing in resilience— the ability to move out of my old harmful habits and into healthier ways of managing emotions.

There is always more work to do in my story, but facing the Coat of Arms assignment made me take a hard, self-reflective look. I needed to answer two questions:

What am I uniquely called to bring to the world?

What has kept me from moving in that direction?

I needed to ask myself some questions. What do I love? Where are my gifts? Will I get caught in the awe of who God created me to be? Discovering themes in my story—performance expectations, self-preservation, and sexual abuse—really stretched my imagination.

Ironically, the ways in which I had learned to survive seemed to become the direction God wanted to point me. My Coat of Arms started to shape into my "stake in the ground." It was time to rewrite the script I long believed and use my heartache and gifts for good.

After an exhaustive Google search, an image of a shield caught my eye. I consider myself to be a novice Adobe Photoshop user, but I popped the program open and stared back at the black, empty outline of the shield.

Bold, strong colors resonated over soft pastels. I filled the upper-left and lower-right quadrants with blue, a shade lighter than navy, to represent my values of truth and loyalty. Loyalty has lived inside me my whole life—at times, even to the point of overpowering truth. The upper-right and lower-left quadrants of the shield I painted green, for the hope brewing inside my heart. I edged the upper and lower border of each section with their opposite color. Green to blue, and blue to green.

The left and right borders of the shield, and the border separating the four quadrants, became white to reflect an awakening of peace in my soul. At the bottom, a banner stretched with the words *Beauty from Ashes* written in Hebrew. A red heart overlapped all four quadrants, with *Alive* written in the center, a marker that my heart pumps with life—I am *strong*.

The upper-left chamber of my shield announced the word *courage*. Dr. Brené Brown defines courage: "To speak one's mind by telling all of one's heart." *When I am afraid, I will do it anyway.* An image of a cross anchored my shield in the lower-right quadrant. My faith and God's Truth sustained me.

Next, I asked myself, *What do I love, and where do my gifts lie?* Sports! It was high time I celebrated the gift God gave me as an athlete and the ability to play at an elite level. Two images—one of a golf ball and another of various sports—added playfulness to the upper-right green area. Part of the vision for my kingdom as a professional golfer would be with golfers and other elite athletes. I *will not be confined to a small piece of soil; I will touch people from around the world,* I told myself.

What am I called to? I was called to offer safe spaces for athletes to talk about their stories of trauma. I was called to offer care and training for sports leaders through individual mentoring, counseling, and small group experiences. Fear and doubt threw their punches, trying to make me believe I was not ready nor did I have something to offer other athletes. I heard a voice telling me to keep performing and hustling for my worth.

No! I was going to choose to enter the war by showing up and offering my presence.

It is enough. I am enough.

Will I get caught in the awe of who God created me to be? My beauty, longings, and desires were good. I was God's beloved. I was an athlete. I was a warrior. I was feminine. I was a woman.

My Coat of Arms was revealing my next step. I was finding my course.

106 // OUT OF THE ROUGH

A year later, the words echoed through the auditorium. "What is the next brave decision you need to make?"

As the conference wrapped up, I felt unresolved in my resolve. I knew I wanted to move forward in offering safe spaces for athletes to talk about their trauma. But ... *how?*

Three possibilities emerged. My heart craved partnering with other people because, most of my life, I have felt alone. Two of my three options pulled me into established non-profit organizations that varied in mission. Becoming part of a staff team felt like being rescued from treading water. The third option was to establish my own nonprofit project under an umbrella foundation. Regardless of which direction I chose, I loathed the idea of fundraising to support my salary and expenses.

Back to my next brave decision.

Out of the Rough Ministries (OOTRM) became a project under The New Horizons Foundation. Yes, slight play on words relating to my golf background: Doing the work to care for one's own story of trauma is like trying to get out of the hard places (rough) and back in the middle of the fairway or onto the green (life). I wanted others to experience what I did and continue on. It is possible to heal, regardless of age or circumstance.

Setting OOTRM as a project under a foundation seemed most logical at this point. It would be less costly, and I didn't have to manage the IRS rules and regulations. I planned to head down this path while I figured out if I wanted to join one of the other two organizations. OOTRM was established as a faith-based organization, but my main goals were not to lead Bible studies. I wanted athletes to know that *their stories mattered—*conversations that I have come to believe need to occur before introducing spiritual conversations.

I stirred the waters in the golf world with my mission. Even though showing up at some of the professional tournaments felt like the first day of school (I was there not to play but to develop relationships), I got my sea legs under me. After a few months, I was able to help a couple players.

Unfortunately, during that time, it also became obvious that one of the two nonprofits I hoped to partner with was a dead end. Disappointment slammed my heart like a rogue wave, and I felt alone again.

The other organization, LINKS Players International, still intrigued me; however, it meant working with a completely different demographic than I had planned to focus on. I had worked with LINKS off and on throughout my golf career, as the subject of interviews, as the author of articles, and even sitting in on board retreat meetings discussing how to encourage more women to become involved in the ministry. Even so, LINKS didn't completely fit my mission of helping elite athletes with their stories of trauma.

Then after months of back-and-forth conversations with the LINKS executive director at the time, Jeff Hopper, we sealed the deal. I became a part-time staff member with LINKS and conducted my direct work with elite athletes through OOTRM. LINKS needed a female presence on their staff, and I believed I could be that woman for a period of time. After experiencing the fruits of my labor by visiting a couple of Ladies Fellowships, I felt wanted, needed, and challenged.

One problem: the two entities started to get entangled. It wasn't working.

When I did events with LINKS, the participants were confused about what I was doing with OOTRM. Jeff and I realized the traction we had hoped for with the women wasn't successful, and, honestly, I never wanted to be the LINKS National Women's Director. It wasn't my calling. I still felt called to play a supporting role to LINKS through writing devotionals, caring for the staff, and contributing to the discussions, but my main purpose remained to mentor and counsel elite athletes and the leaders who served them.

The two years under the LINKS umbrella allowed me time and space to continue to grow and develop as a leader, but I needed a shift in direction.

107 // THE CROSSROADS

I closed the book. Steven Pressfield's words resonated with me.

> The following is a list, in no particular order, of those activities that most commonly elicit Resistance:
> 1) The pursuit of any calling in writing, painting, music, film, dance, or any creative art, however marginal or unconventional.
> 2) The launching of any entrepreneurial venture or enterprise, for profit or otherwise. (Pressfield, *The Art of War* (Black Irish Entertainment), 5.)

I stopped at point no. 2. I had no need to read on.

Letting go of working in partnership with another ministry organization left me disappointed ... *again*. I continued to act in a pseudo-staff role with LINKS and write bimonthly devotionals, but my path forward appeared murky.

Two things became clear, though. My *vision* is, in fact, to help athletes play sports trauma-free, and I can live out this *mission* by providing safe opportunities for elite athletes to talk about their stories of trauma, and training for the leaders who serve them.

My resistance wrestled with the *how*. Doing it on my own feels like facing Mount Everest head-on. The biggest sexual abuse scandal in women's sports was made public first in 2016 by Rachael Denhollander against Michigan State University and Dr. Larry Nassar. Ramifications from this case and others continue to rock the sports world to this day. But the topics of mental and emotional health in the sports world are still touchy. Rachael Denhollander's courage, along with the courage of the hundreds of other victims in gymnastics and other sports, compels me to push forward.

I can't *not* be "all in." Those were the words the Holy Spirit spoke to me for 2017. To do what I believe I'm called to do, even though it seems impossible means I must be *all in*. I had to be willing to totally commit to what was being asked of me.

After several conversations with my fellow board members of an existing 501(c)3 tax-exempt organization which was not currently doing ministry, they agreed to give me the rights to the nonprofit and help me on the path to my vision. All I had to do was work through the process of renaming it *The Tracy Hanson Initiative*. The more simple name, *Out of the Rough Ministries,* served its purpose, but, for my vision and mission to expand, I needed to leverage my reputation as a professional athlete and widen my scope. I hired a lawyer to navigate the paperwork and IRS. Then I waited.

All in.

Five months passed and then I finally received the official paperwork. I formed a Board of Directors and hired a new designer to create a new logo—and a clean, informative website. We landed on a navy and teal color palette that is crisp and inviting. A myriad of hopes and questions collided within me. I was scared and excited at the same time.

What I wasn't excited about was *fundraising*. I wished dollars fell from the sky so all my energy could be funneled into working the mission. But the reality required balancing both fundraising and doing the work. A blessing that comes from building financial and prayer partnerships is the rich relationships that develop with people who believe in me and believe in the work God has given me to do.

During the second half of 2017, I focused on fundraising, building relationships, and slowly developing a program plan for the following year. Our main fundraising event was the Inaugural *The Initiative Pro Am,* featuring my fellow LPGA Tour professionals. We had a great turnout and a profitable day. I played a couple Legends Tour events (now called Legends of the LPGA), connected with several LPGA Tour players, and did a few speaking events with LINKS Players ministry.

"Just keep taking the next right step," I often told myself. Some days ended on a spiritual high after experiencing how God was working in the midst of *The Initiative.* Other days, I slogged through fear and doubt.

Not only did I launch *The Tracy Hanson Initiative* at forty-five years old, I also chose at the same time to return to competitive golf with the *Legends of the LPGA* tour.

108 // WHERE GOLF AND LIFE COLLIDE

The golf club's entryway loomed ahead. I shifted my car into park and surveyed the surroundings. *Will anyone remember me?* I sucked in a deep breath swallowing my uncertainty and headed in to register for my first Legends of the LPGA event.

Legends of the LPGA is the official senior tour that provides competitive opportunities for LPGA Tour members, other professionals, and eligible amateurs over age 45. The tour was founded in 2000 by 25 veteran LPGA Tour professionals with a shared goal of continuing to showcase the talents of the greatest female golfers of all time.

When I retired from the LPGA Tour in 2009, I was done competing—*forever*. Walking into Geneva National Resort, eight years later, was my first attempt at reconsidering that choice. After all of my counseling work, I felt emotionally grounded and mentally ready. It shouldn't be hard to return to competition—or so I thought.

I grabbed my clubs and headed for the putting green. *Will anyone remember me?*

"Tracy Hanson, you're not old enough to be here!" Rosie Jones (13 LPGA Tour career wins) shouted with a big smile.

Other faces looked up and caught my eye. A few came over to welcome me with a hug. A river of relief exhaled out. They *did* remember me.

I survived my first competitive round back alongside my LPGA peers, but it wasn't as easy as I anticipated. I was nervous on every shot. Frustration brewed after missing several short putts. I managed to capture two birdies in my last three holes to finish my roller-coaster round. Rain washed out the second round, making it a one-round event.

As the miles rolled by on my drive home, it hit me. It wasn't my peers who had forgotten me—it was me who had forgotten myself. *I am a golfer.* In all the years that I played on the LPGA Tour, my presence mattered. A more accurate question I needed to face was, *Am I ready to believe in myself and honor my talents as a professional golfer?*

There were several reasons my return to competitive golf didn't go as smoothly as I hoped. I held the same expectations of myself as when I played full-time. It didn't matter that I no longer had the daily repetition of practice or time on the course as I once did. I mistakenly believed that, because I've done years of emotional healing, I would be able to play with freedom. But my body and nervous system still remembered the old patterns of self-contempt and anger.

Many days I really wondered: *Why am I doing this to myself?* But I didn't want to quit. Determined to overcome it, I pressed on.

I continued to keep practicing and playing because golf is part of who I am. I started to enjoy playing social golf. Playing competitively maintained my credibility with other professional athletes. I also started to adjust my perspective towards competitive golf by embracing the process as part of my ongoing healing and growth.

With my return to competitive golf and The Tracy Hanson Initiative gaining traction, my heart stirred towards the young professional golfers on the developmental tour to the LPGA Tour (currently called the EPSON Tour). Resources are minimal on the developmental tour. It's a harsh life. My heartstrings tugged to help them in ways that I had needed help but didn't get at the beginning of my career. Now, with the support of my Board of Directors, I regularly travel to half of the Epson Tour events and offer free emotional and mental health support to these athletes as they pursue their dreams of playing on the LPGA Tour.

While The Initiative is founded on Christian faith, spirituality isn't my starting point with athletes. I want people to know Jesus, but I also believe that I must earn the right to share about the Lord with others by caring for them as human beings first and foremost. My job is to listen well and follow promptings from the Holy Spirit.

There is no manual for the ministry of presence other than being willing to show up.

109 // MY "WHY" IS WORTH IT

When the COVID-19 pandemic hit in 2020, I had just started a Somatic Experiencing (SE) Trauma training program. Peter Levine developed SE to help address the ways in which traumatic stress disrupts the functions of our nervous system. Traditional therapy (talk therapy, story narrative, cognitive behavioral modalities) is considered top-down, but Somatic Experiencing is bottom-up.

The pandemic halted all the momentum I'd gained working with elite athletes. I felt lost. Our SE training moved online, but everything else I had in motion shut down immediately with no ability to travel and no in-person opportunities with athletes. My motivation plummeted.

As the months passed, my personal Somatic therapy sessions revealed just how tired my nervous system was. Decades of travel and high-level competitive stress, along with carrying my hidden trauma for so long, had a high toll. While the pandemic shut down forced physical rest, I also realized my therapeutic journey was not done.

As trauma expert Peter A. Levine teaches, trauma causes a loss of connection over time to the world, to families, to ourselves and to our bodies. Gradually our self-esteem, confidence, and well-being erode, and we keep it all hidden.

Truth be told, we never fully arrive in a state of mental, emotional, and spiritual completion on this side of heaven. The journey is ongoing. Every day, I want to grow and learn more about myself. My nervous system is still healing, and that is okay.

As I finish writing this book, the COVID-19 pandemic is more than four years behind us. My mission to provide safe opportunities for elite athletes to talk about their trauma is back in full gear. Sports leaders are filling our Story Group retreats, preparing themselves to better support the athletes they serve. My competitive playing opportunities are on the rise, and I have renewed energy to work on my golf game.

As former professional baseball player and author Jim Murphy wrote in his book *Inner Excellence* (2020), "I compete to raise the level of excellence in my life, to learn and grow, in order to raise it in others."

I am saying "yes" to this kind of inner excellence and a wholehearted life, and I invite you to do the same.

We all have a story that matters—one that is worthy to be told and heard. When we bear witness with one another, we find our course together. A course that leads to healing, hope, and purpose.

As my story continues to blossom in truth and understanding, I say "Hell no!" to the Thief (evil) who, as the Bible says in John 10:10, comes to "steal and kill and destroy."

Now in my fifth decade, my life is not exactly what I thought it would be. I thought I would be married, but I'm not. I didn't have my own children, but I love being Aunt Tracy to my two nieces and nephew and to friends' children. Life is hard and it is good.

Through my journey, from pain to purpose, I know one thing: If I have the chance to help even one person, I'll keep finding my course. It is worth the fight.

Staring down an iron shot on the LPGA Tour somewhere in 2007.

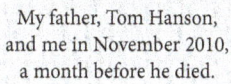

My father, Tom Hanson, and me in November 2010, a month before he died.

Since 2017 I've returned to playing on the Legends of the LPGA and finding joy in the game again.

Speaking at a Tracy Hanson Initiative Pro-Am, an annual event to raise funds for The Initiative's programs.

A champion again, at the 2023 South Carolina Women's Senior Open, a return to feeling like I still belong in competitive golf.

The toddler on the mono-bike grew up but still loves motorcycles. My 2005 Honda Shadow, my adult hobby.

With Kay Agal, still a part of my life more than a decade after she first pursued my heart and encouraged me to get help.

APPENDIX A

There is an undeniable problem of abuse or mistreatment in sports and it impacts athletes of all levels. Abuse occurs relationally in four categories: sexual, physical, psychological, and emotional. It also happens in the context of "non-critical relationships" between athletes and educational institutions, owners and management of professional teams, medical staff, or even fans.

I would like to speak to three groups of people: athletes, parents and guardians, and coaches and sports administrators.

A Note to Athletes

I wrote my story for you. Regardless of what level of sport you play, you are a human being with dignity and choice. No coach or authority figure has the right to take that from you.

If you have experienced abuse in any form—verbal, physical, emotional, spiritual, or sexual—I am heartbroken for and with you. If you have told a safe person about your harm, I applaud you. If you have not, I know there are reasons.

During the real time of being groomed over a four-year period, I had no context to help me understand that I could tell someone what was happening. I believed I had to keep the secret. Today I understand how scared I must have been, how I believed I was at fault, and how my future dreams would have been in jeopardy if I would have told.

When we don't get the help we need, the impacts of abuse and shame are carried in our bodies and will sprout into real emotional and physical problems over time. I hope you will seek out the help you need either through a good therapist or a safe person.

Three helpful books to begin are:

> *The Body Keeps The Score: Brain, Mind, and Body in the Healing of Trauma* by Bessel Van Der Kolk, M.D. (Penguin Books, 2014).

> *The Soul of Shame: Retelling the Stories We Believe About Ourselves* by Curt Thompson, M.D. (IVP Press, 2015).

> *Make Sense of Your Story: Why Engaging Your Past with Kindness Changes Everything* by Adam Young (Baker Books, 2025).

A Note to Parents and Guardians

Being a parent is a great responsibility. Being a sports parent is doubly hard. On one hand, children are dependent on you to guide, emotionally regulate, and encourage them to explore the world. At the same time, you will have to decide to trust your children to coaches and sports organizations along the way.

Most sexual abuse survivors know the person who assaulted them. The perpetrator may be a family member, a coach, a caregiver, friend, or an acquaintance. Symptoms to be aware of are depression, anxiety, a sudden change in behavior or mood, a lack of interest in activities, a drop in academic results, or a sudden increase or decrease of weight (not an exhaustive list).

Whether your child is still participating in sports or not, it is never too late to pursue an open dialogue about his or her sport experiences.

A Note to Coaches and Sports Administrators

You have the opportunity to positively affect athletes' development physically, mentally, and emotionally. The pressure to succeed—whether it be in youth, college, or professional sports—is weighty. I imagine it can feel impossible at times to meet the expectations demanded of you. In the midst of these demands, it is still your responsibility to provide an environment that is safe for your staff and athletes.

Athletes look to you for guidance and help in reaching their full potential. I encourage you to never stop pursuing your own personal growth and development as a leader. Results and accomplishments are great, and they should never trump the well-being of any athlete.

John Wooden, long-time coach at UCLA, said, "Be more concerned with your character than your reputation, because your character is what you really are, while your reputation is merely what others think you are."

APPENDIX B

"WHY JESUS?"*

I struggle to find adequate words to describe an answer to the question, Why Jesus? I personally recoil at anything that sounds too "churchy." And yet, there is a truth to be told.

God's original desire in creating Adam and Eve, the first humans in God's image, was for relationship. God gave them freedom in the perfect world in which they lived. Except for one rule, "You may surely eat of every tree of the garden, but of the tree of the knowledge of good and evil you shall not eat…" (Genesis 2:17).

But another presence within their midst, Satan, whispered doubt into their minds and ultimately their hearts. They ate of the very tree that God said to stay away from. Their relationship with their Creator, with creation, and with each other, was broken.

The consequence of Adam and Eve's failure left all human beings with an internal void that resembles the missing piece of a jigsaw puzzle.

This human condition, along with the reality that we can never be "good enough" or "do enough" to fill this void, is a separated relationship from God. But God, the Creator, provided a way for all human beings to be reunited with Him here on earth and for all eternity through his Son Jesus.

According to Scripture, the only righteousness that counts before God is the perfect righteousness of Jesus, who is the promised Messiah called "the Christ" (meaning anointed one).

Jesus is pursuing each one of our hearts. He wants to be in relationship with each one of us, and to do his transformative work in reuniting us to God, the Father.

If we are to enter God's presence for eternity, we will do so only by placing our faith and trust in Jesus. "If you declare with your mouth, 'Jesus is Lord,' and believe in your heart that God raised him from the dead, you will be saved" (Romans 10:9).

When we make the choice to follow Jesus, the missing jigsaw puzzle piece is found and the picture of one's life becomes complete.

From LINKS Players International. Used with permission.

APPENDIX C

"FOR MOM"

We never thought this day would come so fast
You fought hard to the very last
We are feeling such a loss, but you have only gained
You are with God in glory forever today

A faithful, devoted wife
A caring, loving mother full of life
You loved us unconditionally through thick and thin
With you by our side we could only win

You will be missed more than words can say
You loved us all in your own silent way
Your smile and touch came straight from the heart
God will take care of us while we're apart

You were strong, independent, and witty too
Each one of us found a friend in you
You always did so much that we neglected to see
You have inspired us to become everything we can be

Now we will let you go and set you free
For you are in a better place shouting with glee
Your pain is gone and God has brought you home
Never again will you be alone

We thank our God in Heaven for each memory of you
Our hearts can smile because we saw Him in you
We thank our God in Heaven for each memory of you
You have shown us that God's love is ever so True

APPENDIX D

A GLOSSARY FOR NON-GOLFERS

Standard Golf Course: 18 holes, split into a front 9 holes and a back 9 holes.

Par: the standard number of strokes needed for a hole.

Par 3: a hole where three strokes equals a par.

Par 4: a hole where four strokes equals a par.

Par 5: a hole where five strokes equals a par.

Birdie: one stroke under par for a hole.

Eagle: two strokes under par for a hole.

Double Eagle: three strokes under par for a hole (on a par 5).

Bogie: one stroke over par for a hole.

Double Bogie: two strokes over par for a hole.

Triple Bogie: three strokes over par for a hole.

Tee Box: the area defined for where the first stroke is taken on a hole.

Green: the area at the far end of a golf hole where the grass is kept shorter and a golfer is meant to use a putter.

Hole: a circular hole made in the green for the ball to finish and end the hole.

Tee Stroke or Drive: the first stroke taken on any given hole.

Approach Shot: a stroke taken towards the green.

Lay-Up: a stroke taken on any hole (most often on a par 5) to position the golfer for the next stroke.

Putt: a stroke made on the green to cause the ball to roll near or in the hole.

Hook: for a right-handed golfer, a curve of the ball that moves from the right to the left. For a left-handed golfer, a curve of the ball that moves from the left to the right.

Slice: for a right-handed golfer, a curve of the ball that moves from left to right. For a left-handed golfer, a curve of the ball that moves from right to left.

Divot: a patch of turf cut out of the ground by a golf club during a stroke.

Whiff: missing the golf ball during an intentional stroke.

Bunker: a hazard that is a depression in the ground and filled with sand.

Out of Bounds: outside the playing area on a golf course.

Caddie: a person who carries a player's golf bag and provides on-course support and guidance.

Tee Time: the designated time for a golfer to start his or her round of golf.

ACKNOWLEDGMENTS

Writing my story has been an experience of starts and stops. It's been both laborious and full of blessings. When friends and mentors suggested I needed to write my story, I looked at them like they were crazy. When God started nudging me to write, I was resistant. In the end, more than a decade later, I have grown, been challenged, and learned through the process.

Thank you to my Lord and Savior Jesus. My spiritual relationship has followed highs and lows and you have always remained faithful.

I would not have a final manuscript without the support of my family, friends, counselors, editors, mentors, and financial partners.

To my family, Eddie, Debbie, Rich, Haley, Courtney, and André: you have supported and loved me through the life we share. Thank you for being my people. Love you to the moon and back.

I wouldn't know that my story was worth my attention without three women: Amy, Kay, and Tracy. Thank you for seeing me, challenging me to seek truth, and for guiding me along on my journey. To Maria (AKA Loopy), Heidi, Angel, Mama Dora, you have known the good, the hard, the ugly, and the beautiful pieces of my life. Thank you for remaining faithful through the decades. Janet, Liane, Ann, Rhonda, Carla, Sharon, and Mindy you have been ears that have listened, offered encouragement when I needed it, brought out my playful side, and allowed me to be me.

I am also grateful to the men who have loved me well and walked with me through the hard places of my story. You have given me the gift of feeling safe, seen and delighted in.

To LINKS Players International, thank you for embracing me and loving me like family. I am grateful to be a part of your mission to change the conversation in the golf community.

Thank you to The Tracy Hanson Initiative financial partners who have supported my vision and mission to help athletes play and live free of trauma. I would not be able to complete this project without you.

A huge thank you to my creative editors and book designers, Lauren Befus, Anita Palmer, Chris Gettle, and Design9Studios, who have led me through the process of creating a book. You pushed and challenged me in so many honorable ways. You have helped bring my story to these pages and I am grateful.

ABOUT THE AUTHOR

Tracy Hanson grew up in Northern Idaho, where she developed a love for sports and excelled in basketball and golf. She was recruited to play collegiate golf at San Jose State University, After graduation she embarked on a successful 15-year career on the LPGA Tour.

Tracy's life journey took a transformative turn when she sought counseling to heal from sexual abuse and trauma. Through her healing, she discovered a calling to help others, particularly athletes navigating similar challenges. She founded The Tracy Hanson Initiative, where she supports and guides others through their journeys. Tracy also is a certified Lay Counselor from The Allender Center and a Somatic Experiencing Practitioner, and speaker.

She is also a Legends of the LPGA Professional and regularly writes for the Links Players Daily Devotional, inspiring readers with her faith and wisdom.

When she's not writing or helping others, Tracy enjoys riding motorcycles, hiking, and working out, finding joy and adventure in life's simple pleasures. She resides in Michigan.

ABOUT THE TRACY HANSON INITIATIVE

The Tracy Hanson Initiative exists to empower elite athletes to live and play free from the effects of trauma experienced in sports, and to train coaches, sports chaplains, and other leaders in the sports world on how to better help their athletes emotionally, mentally, and spiritually.

Initiative programs include individual mentoring and counseling, presentations, and story group retreats. Through the Initiative, Tracy Hanson speaks at women's and men's events, sports camps, church gatherings, and pro-am charity events, and appears on a variety of podcasts.

The Initiative's key values are compassion, hope, honesty, kindness, and confidentiality.

For more information, visit https://tracyhanson.com.

www.ingramcontent.com/pod-product-compliance
Lightning Source LLC
Chambersburg PA
CBHW040309170426
43195CB00020B/2901